FAMILY MEDIATION CASEBOOK
Theory and Process

FRONTIERS IN COUPLES AND FAMILY THERAPY
A Brunner/Mazel Book Series

Series Editor: Florence W. Kaslow, Ph.D.

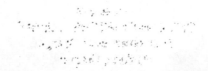

FAMILY MEDIATION CASEBOOK

Theory and Process

By

Stephen K. Erickson &
Marilyn S. McKnight Erickson

BRUNNER/MAZEL *Publishers* • New York

Library of Congress Cataloging-in-Publication Data

Erickson, Stephen K.
    Family mediation casebook : theory and process / by Stephen K.
Erickson & Marilyn S. McKnight Erickson.
        p.   cm.—(Frontiers in couples and family therapy)
    Bibliography: p.
    Includes index.
    ISBN 0-87630-525-7
    1. Divorce mediation—United States—Case studies.   2. Family
psychotherapy—United States—Case studies.   3. Family mediation—
United States—Case studies.   I. Erickson, Marilyn S. McKnight.
II. Title.   III. Series.
HQ834.E75 1988   88-15026
306.8'9—dc19   CIP

Copyright © 1988 by Brunner/Mazel, Inc.

Published by
BRUNNER/MAZEL, INC.
19 Union Square
New York, New York 10003

MANUFACTURED IN THE UNITED STATES OF AMERICA

10 9 8 7 6 5 4 3 2 1

Contents

Preface

The Ericksons' many years of experience as mediation trainers and "hands-on" mediators shine through in this lucid, clear exposition of mediation theory, content, and process. This book contains a straightforward, unembellished articulation of the "how to" of family and divorce mediation, enabling the reader to bring it to successful conclusion; emphasis on process and technique is amply illustrated by case presentations and analyses.

The authors provide a well-thought-out discussion of the differences between mediation and counseling, and throughout the book, in their exposition of the mediation process, make clear how this differs from the adversarial process.

Another salient discussion revolves around power: who has it, how it is manifested or kept covert, and the differences in strengths and weaknesses of the parting spouses, as these almost float back and forth, depending on the issue under consideration. The authors highlight their understanding of a person's attempts to break free from a destructive relationship and the reasons that underlie attempts to gain power. In this useful section (Chapter 7), the reader can see how they tease out the often-hidden rules and establish their own, such as "Speak only for yourself and in first person" (i.e., make "I" and not accusatory "you" statements) and "Follow any criticism with a positive suggestion." The reader senses that they are *strong* mediators in the most positive connotation of *strong* (i.e., decisive, competent, and assertively in charge of facilitating the mediation process).

The discussion of mediating *spousal abuse cases* is particularly valuable and quite fascinating. Whenever I have done a basic mediation training, the question arises: If there is an allegation of child or spouse abuse, are we obligated, as mental health and lawyer mediators, to report the allegation to the proper authorities? This is a critical and perplexing dilemma. The Ericksons discuss how this should be handled, with a definite preference for self-reporting the implications for the mediation. They take us through the procedures and process step by step, providing a fine protocol for adaptation and use by readers. They express concern about the impact of the abuse on the children, whether it is spouse to spouse or parent to child, the importance of protecting children from future abuse, and the issues of confidentiality as they intertwine with the legal mandate to report. I found this one of the most significant portions of the book; the authors ask and answer the hard questions.

The Ericksons make it clear that mediators cannot beg the issue and that in addition to reporting the allegation, they refer such cases for therapy, making that a condition for them to continue with the mediation. This strong stance is typical of their modus operandi; as in family therapy, they believe that it is important for the mediator to, as Whitaker says, "win the battle for structure." They accomplish this by firmly establishing the rules and seeing that they are followed.

The many cases described in this volume cover a wide range of problems. In one case, parent versus grandparent concerns are highlighted; in another, the importance of a definite schedule for visitation (exchange) of children to permit all parties involved a high level of predictability in their lives and the ability to plan is underscored; and in a third, there is a touching account of a review session with children, set up to help them achieve clarity about and closure over what is transpiring.

Throughout, the authors profess and adhere to a structured problem-solving process that is goal-oriented to lead toward the best possible agreement for the specific couple or family. Once they assist the party who feels rejected to accept the divorce decision, they keep their mediations present- and future-oriented and block out efforts to rehash the past. If the parties need to do this, this aspect of the work is properly referred to a therapist. They help the parties negotiate and compromise, not threaten or intimidate. The Ericksons provide data that validate an assumption in the field; when couples arrive at their own agreements, about which they are proud, they have a much greater stake in implementing them and seeing that they work.

As the authors spell out the multifaceted and complex role of the mediator, the reader becomes aware of why those engaged in this role should be seasoned, mature professionals with an in-depth understanding of family dynamics, child development, the impact of divorce on all involved, as well as budgeting, property distribution and the accompanying tax ramifications, child and spousal support, and so forth. Specific training in divorce mediation, above and beyond one's graduate or professional training as a mental health professional or attorney, emerges as crucial, as does the need for ongoing continuing education to remain abreast of changes in relevant laws and consultation on difficult cases.

The final chapter, "Strategies to Avoid Impasse," speaks to another concern often expressed by mediators. The Ericksons' delineation of numerous techniques that they use to avoid impasse is crystal clear; after reading this, the reader can quickly attempt to utilize some or all of these techniques with their most recalcitrant clients and may feel better equipped to deal with overly zealous litigators.

I believe this book is destined to become a classic in the mediation field and will be used as a text in law school and mental health classes, as well as in specialized mediation training programs. Practicing mediation professionals will also find its practical guidelines and case examples invaluable in their own work. For these reasons I am particularly pleased to have this volume as part of the Series, *Frontiers in Couples and Family Therapy.*

March 1988   Florence W. Kaslow, Ph.D.
                                                      Series Editor
                                Florida Couples and Family Institute
                                             West Palm Beach, FL

Introduction

Mediation in the United States was once considered the province of labor and union mediators who discovered in the late 1930s and in the 1940s that it was far more effective to resolve disputes at the bargaining table than in the streets. In the early 1970s an attorney, Jim Coogler, decided to apply the mediation process to couples in the midst of divorce. Since his early work, there has indeed been a great rush to promote the use of mediation for divorcing families. An indication of the growth of family mediation is evidenced by the proliferation of laws encouraging divorce and custody mediation. In 1979 I began work on a Fellowship by examining the statutes of all 50 states in an effort to find laws relating to mediation. At that time, the only references to mediation were the enabling laws creating a small number of state mediation bureaus. The purpose of these state offices was to coordinate the mediation process for certain groups of state workers such as teachers, police, and firefighters, who were required to mediate before striking. Within the span of just 10 years, virtually every state in the United States, as well as Canada and other countries, has enacted laws or is considering legislation to promote the use of mediation between divorcing couples.

Why this sudden growth of interest in something that has been around since New Testament times? (The apostle Paul encouraged the use of mediation in the early Christian church to settle differences rather than resorting to the Roman court system.) The simple and probably best answer is that it works and it works exceedingly well. A more complex answer might cite the public's growing dissatisfaction with the adversarial process. Another answer might discuss the mental health profession's research findings which indicate that children of divorce are harmed more by their parents' conflict than by any other single factor. Whatever the answer, the purpose of this book is not to discuss the *why* of divorce mediation, but rather the *how* of divorce mediation. That is, the cases in this book, together with the chapters on conceptual framework, power analysis, and impasse strategies, provide the reader with a practical glimpse into the actual working process of mediation between divorcing couples.

We developed our unique method of mediation first as a reaction to the excesses of the adversarial process and second as a systematic method of peacemaking. It must be remembered that the word *mediation* does not imply a universal method followed by all. Indeed, many things that are called mediation these days are little more than competitive negotiations in the guise of mediation. We believe our conceptual framework is useful because it attempts to provide the reader with specific methods to counter each element of the adversarial process with an opposite intervention in order to create all of the elements necessary for cooperative problem resolution.

This book grew out of our teaching and training activities and our efforts at successfully mediating over 1,000 cases during a period of 10 years. Some couples who mediated with us were exceedingly wealthy; others were exceedingly poor, with the wife on welfare and the husband unemployed. In all of these cases, the same process was used with the same degree of success. During the past 10 years, approximately 90% of the couples who started in mediation with us reached a complete agreement that was later approved and implemented by the couple's individual attorneys. Approximately 10% of the couples either dropped out of mediation or reached impasse.

The case examples in this volume are presented to show the application of the conceptual framework as carried out in the mediation room. These cases were mediated by one or both of the authors during the preceeding 11 years. The names used are not real names, and other identifying information has been significantly changed to assure confidentiality and anonymity.

In attempting to present the reader with insight about the process, we divided the work of writing this book. In some chapters we collaborated; in others we reported on our own cases. Therefore, the reader may note that there is a degree of inconsistency between the use of "I" and "we" when referring to the mediator. Although the two of us seldom co-mediate as a team, we have become so used to working together that even in this book we cannot distinguish between our individual ideas and our joint ideas. Therefore, the reader is asked to assume that a single mediator is present in each case. When the commentary about the process refers to "we," this represents our joint ideas and observations.

We could list endlessly those whom we feel are responsible for helping the concept grow. Certainly Jim Coogler and Judge Jack Etheridge of Atlanta helped so much in those early years when everybody was saying it was a nice idea, but it wouldn't work. Virginia Stafford, Will Neville, John Haynes, Joan Kelly, Burt Zoub, Dudley Flanders, Emily Brown, and Mark Lohman, to mention a few, are part of the "old-timers' " group who all swam upstream together and demonstrated in those early years of the late 1970s and early 1980s that divorce mediation was more than a fad. Without the help and encouragement from leaders in other fields such as Larry Ray of the American Bar Association and, of course, Florence Kaslow, it would have been difficult to advance the concept beyond a small group of practitioners. In our own state of Minnesota, we must acknowledge A. M. "Sandy" Keith as one of the most enlightened supporters, whose help and encouragement gave us strength to succeed when the odds appeared overwhelming.

Looking to the future, we must learn to think of divorce as a family problem, not a legal problem. It has become a legal problem only because we have required families to submit to the degrading and often humiliating procedures of changed locks on the doors, ex parte restraining orders, depositions, custody studies, and other "invasive" procedures. In the name of justice, our system asks a husband to stand quietly by while the attorney alleges that his wife is lazy, unmotivated and surely capable of finding work if only she weren't so intent upon getting a free ride from him. We require a wife to hire advocates to find out financial information that should have been shared information, but now becomes the scraps from the table in the final battle over who will get the gold mine and who will get the shaft. We require judges to be Solomon-like even though they are only human. We require attorneys to be zealous advocates who become so fearful of malpractice lawsuits that they must search under every stone to make sure that they have not missed some item that may later come back to haunt them.

We have created an environment where some psychologists and other experts become "hired guns" for the side paying their fee in a custody battle. We have created a national disgrace, and the only people complaining about it are the victims of the process—those husbands and wives who are trapped by an antiquated system of conflict resolution that teaches people to believe that the only way they can get their needs met is to view their spouses as the root cause of all their own problems. Mental health experts tell us this is an unhealthy and destructive way of ending a relationship.

We have not heeded the advice of the experts. We have failed the children of divorce miserably. We continue to treat them as property when, in fact, they are innocent victims. When the court system should be encouraging parents to act more responsibly, we say that the only thing the court can do is decide who will own the children. Our current laws encourage a battle, but we should direct our energy toward more productive work, such as demanding and then helping the couple to learn more cooperative ways of engaging each other as single parents.

This book is our attempt to create a new environment where all our efforts are directed toward teaching peaceful, cooperative solutions rather than encouraging people to wage destructive divorce wars.

March 1988   Stephen K. Erickson
Marilyn S. McKnight Erickson
Minneapolis, MN

1

A Conceptual Framework of Divorce Mediation

Although much has been published in the last 10 years about divorce mediation, few have tried to explain in detail the actual mechanics of the process. This book attempts to provide the reader with both a theoretical framework and a look at how the theory is applied to actual cases mediated successfully.

Conceptual frameworks have always been helpful in describing a theory or explaining a complex idea. Were we to know all there is to know about teaching people to cooperate, this world would be a very different place to live. Although we still have a great deal to learn, the following ideas emerge from our experience during the past 11 years, as well as from the existing research and literature on conflict resolution.

Mediation, particularly family mediation, is easy to describe in a few words. It is a communication process by which a husband and wife resolve the practical and the emotional issues of divorce or separation in a mutual, cooperative manner as opposed to an adversarial, competitive manner. Using a neutral mediator to guide the couple's communication, mediation allows couples to make the best possible decisions in the settlement of their divorce, even though they may be in great turmoil and conflict. Given the two parties' different values, different abilities and limited resources to face the future, mediation provides a participatory process for them to achieve a successful termination of a partnership that has created children, shared income and accumulated assets. The goal is for each of them to receive the best settlement possible that will satisfy to the greatest extent possible their respective needs and interests, now and in the future.

Although the couple may be highly conflicted, the goal of mediation is to prevent the conflict from becoming destructive. Conflict is always painful: "Conflict is among the most common causes of long-term, severe suffering because nowhere do we lose more control than when we are in true conflict" (Glasser, 1984, p. 149). When a husband and wife divorce, the pain of the conflict can become infinitely damaging to the entire family.

Unfortunately, as a society we have given little assistance to families in divorce and in most cases we have unknowingly generated more harm and pain through our adversarial system of justice. In fact, our society has constructed a legal remedy for resolving the divorce conflict that is completely antithetical to basic mental health principles. "The successful divorce should also leave each partner with a balanced view of the other and of the marriage, and with a sense of psychological closure" (Kressel, 1985, p. 77). The adversarial system accomplishes neither goal. At the point couples embark on the process of separation and divorce, society advises them to get a zealous attorney to protect themselves. In order to be successful in an adversarial divorce, couples learn to view their spouse as an adversary, resulting in a billion-dollar industry that often generates even more conflict and pain for the couple and their children. Because the nature of the adversarial system requires zealous representation, an attorney who might wish to take a balanced view of the other side may be accused of providing weak and ineffective representation. Unfortunately, the net result of a lawyer's representation is often exacerbation of the conflict rather than psychological closure.

Divorce mediation is an attempt to establish a more humane, cooperative approach to divorce settlement. This is consistent with the objectives of mental health practitioners who assert that couples must move beyond pain, anger and mistrust in order to achieve a satisfactory resolution of the divorce experience. As will be seen by the case examples, mediated divorces promise to be less painful and more protective of the "needs" of couples in the midst of divorce.

Many conceptual frameworks can be summarized in a single phrase, such as systems theory, symbolic interactionism, problem-solving therapy, or other descriptive words that capture the theory. The term "process theory" is chosen to describe our conceptual framework of mediation based upon the belief that a set of fair procedural steps, coupled with application of many techniques pioneered by mental health professionals, results in a pro-

cess that inevitably moves the couple towards cooperative choices and tolerable solutions.

The process of family mediation provides an orderly
manner for couples to begin to achieve wholeness after
the emotional and financial chaos of terminating the marriage relationship because it does not require each spouse
to view the other as an adversary. In addition, a corner-
stone of the theory is that people achieve quicker, wiser
and more lasting results when they are encouraged to
make their own decisions about the termination of the
marital partnership than if others make choices for them.

Unfortunately, most couples are unable to sit down
around the kitchen table and make good decisions about
children, money and property without professional help.
This is because emotions are so intense during the divorce that their decision-making process gets contami-
nated by the emotional overlay. Indeed, researchers have
shown that the mental health effects of divorce and separation are overwhelming (Barker, 1984, p. 21). Tradition-
ally, couples have turned to therapists for help with the
emotions and to lawyers for help with the decisions to be
made affecting the material things of the marriage (including children).

With the emergence of family mediation, couples may
now use one professional mediator to assist with the resolution of the material things of the marriage; in that process the emotions are often improved. Indeed, the process theory of divorce mediation argues that it is always
therapeutic to create order and certainty out of chaos and
confusion. For many couples, the cooperative decision
making involved in divorce mediation is enough therapy
in itself to get them through the business of finishing the
stages of the emotional divorce. For others, a referral to
a qualified therapist may be necessary to keep the media-

tion negotiations from becoming negatively affected by intense emotions. In such cases, the processes of mediation and therapy occur simultaneously and greatly complement each other.

The building blocks of this conceptual framework are observed in the way a mediator influences four aspects of the negotiations. These are: (1) communication; (2) attitudes; (3) negotiating methods; and (4) outcome goals. To understand the conceptual framework of family mediation, it is important to analyze each part of the process and compare it with the adversarial framework of a litigated or lawyer-negotiated divorce. The following, then, is a description of the four areas a mediator tries to influence so as to create a cooperative settlement outcome.

1. COMMUNICATION

Open and Honest Rather Than Guarded, Secretive or Deceptive Communication

A professional family mediator will have clearly in mind the skills needed to influence healthy communication. Bolton (1979) outlines many of the basic tenets of what the mediator must do in this phase of the process. He states that open, honest communication, with an absence of blaming and fault-finding, is essential to maintaining a healthy relationship. Researcher Morton Deutsch (1973) looked not at marriage relationships but rather at the bargaining and negotiation processes and reached a similar conclusion about communication. He argued that cooperative negotiations also required an environment where the communication patterns were open and honest and contained little or no blaming or fault-finding (pp. 351–400).

Successful divorce mediation requires intervention skills that diminish or eliminate the need to be guarded, secretive or deceptive in communications between the parties. This is often difficult, because they may have previously retained an attorney who has urged each of them to be wary of disclosing anything material to the other and the attorney may even have strongly advised the couple to avoid speaking to each other. This is certainly good advice if the decisions are going to be resolved in the competitive atmosphere of the courthouse (or the courthouse steps). However, we have learned from the mental health profession that good marriages are based upon open and honest communication. We know from Deutsch and from our own experience with couples who achieve success in divorce mediation that open and honest communication is one of the first prerequisites to successful resolution of the concrete issues of divorce.

Mediators create the environment for open and honest communication by establishing formal (see Appendix A) and informal rules which include:

1. **Confidentiality** that prohibits the use of mediation discussions in the adversarial process, and also commits each to not discuss what is happening in mediation with others outside the room except by prior agreement. Confidentiality also respects their privacy in mediation and does not allow the mediator to discuss their mediation with others unless written permission is obtained from both parties.

2. **Full disclosure** assures each of them that they will mediate with full and complete information about all assets, liabilities and other information pertinent to the settlement of their divorce.

3. **Speak for yourself** using "I" statements that do not

include statements about or in place of the other party to the mediation.

4. **Speak in positive language** that does not allow for disparaging remarks aimed at the other party, either explicitly or implicitly.

These rules lay the groundwork for open, honest discussion of all of the issues without harm, secrets or deception. They are intended to ensure an atmosphere of emotional safety, as well as to promote direct communication.

Some family law attorneys maintain that only the power of the court can compel honesty. This is false; in fact, obtaining necessary facts about assets and finances in an adversarial manner actually creates the environment for dishonesty and unwillingness to disclose by imposing a competitive process that encourages vigorous attempts to "win" the conflict. Frequently, the unwillingness to disclose in a litigating forum results from fear and frustration with the process. Skilled family mediators have been able to mediate even the most complex divorce cases involving several million dollars in property assets using the process theory approach to mediation. There is no need to assume that only custody matters should be submitted to mediation. However, a mediator must be aware of the need to be detailed and demanding when helping the couple identify and value their assets.

Persuasive Rather Than Coercive Communication

Deutsch (1973) observes that destructive conflict is characterized by a tendency to expand and escalate (p. 351). Also, he notes: "Paralleling the expansion of the scope of conflict, there is an increasing reliance upon a strategy of power and upon the tactics of threat, coercion, and deception. Correspondingly, there is a shift away from a strategy of persuasion and from the tactics of conciliation, minimization of differences and enhancement of mutual understanding and goodwill" (p. 352).

In the process theory of mediation, the mediator's technique of immediately intervening to prohibit coercive communication statements and patterns has the effect of reversing the escalation of the conflict. Efforts at teaching the couple to communicate in a persuasive manner further create an environment where cooperation can occur.

Listening skills are another basic tool to encourage persuasive communication. Any statement made by a party that contains a threat or an "if . . ., then . . ." sequence will be noted by the mediator as not being helpful to the process. The mediator may then ask for a restatement or may even rephrase what is being said in order to understand the underlying need expressed by the person. Indeed, many facial expressions observed in the mediation room evidencing anger or hostility are often preceded by the other party communicating in a threatening or coercive manner. Parties are taught by the mediator that it is easier for them to get their needs met through persuasive communication rather than by coercion.

Little or No Blaming or Fault-Finding as Opposed to Finding Fault in Order to Prove One's Case

Mediators try to reduce or eliminate blaming and fault-finding. Litigators use fault-finding as a way to win their cases. It is still the law in Louisiana that if an attorney can show that the wife engaged in adulterous behavior or other conduct that would entitle a husband to obtain a legal separation, during marriage or the period of separation, she is not entitled to receive spousal support (Louisiana Civil Code, Article 160). Moreover, in every state, in order to win custody or a higher level of ownership of the children, one must show that the other parent engaged (or will engage) in faulty parenting as compared to one's own parenting abilities.

Process theory mediators assume that both parents are significant to the children as parents and that the goal is not to spend thousands to prove who was the worst parent in the past, but to define the shape of the parenting relationship of each parent in the future. Parents in mediation will learn how to make agreements and carry them out over a period of time so that each parent can be the good, loving parent he or she wishes to be. Such learning cannot occur in an atmosphere of blame and fault-finding.

Mediators minimize blaming and fault finding communication patterns by using several methods. First, the couple is asked to agree that such communication does not enhance the process, but rather detracts from a successful mediation process. Second, the mediator redefines the issues in such a way as to require mutual positive work to answer the question, rather than asking the question in such a way as to require a good-bad examination. Third, mediators use skills and techniques to focus the couple on the future rather than on the past.

In the process theory of divorce mediation, the mediator must also be able to influence the attitudes of the parties in order to achieve a successful, cooperative outcome. Thus, the intervention used by the mediator in such a way as to change attitudes becomes the second major aspect of the conceptual framework.

2. ATTITUDES

Create Trust, Rather Than Encourage Mistrust and Suspicion

Experts on cooperative conflict resolution methods stress the importance of creating trust and attitudes of mutuality. The problem for couples in the midst of divorce is to help them find the concrete agreements both can make in order to begin experiencing a measure of trust in the other.

We have frequently been asked by media representatives, "How can you possibly expect a husband and wife to sit down to the mediation table and work out their divorce—aren't they ready to kill each other?" Mediators understand that when a couple decides to divorce, they are perhaps at the most highly conflicted point in their entire lives. Yet it does not make sense to say to them, "You each need to get a strong, aggressive attorney and spend the next 18 months trying to prove that the other is the root cause of all your problems." It is much wiser from both a commonsense as well as a mental health viewpoint to encourage a change of attitude so productive interaction as separate parents in the future will occur. As idealistic as this may sound, all couples indicate a preference for divorcing with dignity.

Divorce mediators and most mental health professionals agree that in order for the couple to carry on separate parenting after the divorce, they must have some measure of trust or they will never be able to effectively exchange the children and communicate about all the joint issues that arise when parenting the children from separate homes. Divorce mediators also know that good negotiations require an element of trust in order to be successfully concluded and implemented.

Therefore, mediators create an attitude of trust by first assuming that all people are capable of giving and receiving trust and then by asking the couple to begin the process of rebuilding trust. This is done by selecting small, manageable areas of decision making, asking them to agree, and then helping them carry out these small agreements between sessions.

However, divorce mediators are not naive. Just like the attorneys who require that every substantive fact in the divorce be shown by documentary evidence, the mediator requests the same verification of income, property, bank accounts and other assets in order to establish truth and thereby diminish any attitudes of mistrust and suspicion.

Mutuality Rather Than Individualistic Attitudes

In a competitive or adversarial game, each side tries to achieve victory over the other. In litigated and in adversarial negotiated divorces, each side develops an attitude that says: "I can get the things I need for myself only at the expense of my spouse. And since my spouse is trying to get or keep as much as possible, I must think only of myself if I am to come out of this divorce intact." In mediation, the couple is encouraged to think of themselves as "in the soup together," sharing the problems to be solved. They are asked to develop an attitude that says: "I am able to get the things I need for myself only if my spouse and my children are able to get the things they also need for their separate future."

Mediators accomplish this task through several techniques. First, the couple is reminded that in mediation it is possible for each to get his or her needs met. Second, the mediator listens closely to their discussions about complaints and attempts to point out areas where they can get their own needs met only if the other cooperates. A dependent wife can become independent only if she receives spousal support from her husband for a period of time. A husband earning three times as much as his wife can expect to become financially independent only if he helps her to achieve the tools and education she may need to improve her income. Likewise, if she is trying to become financially independent of him, he must be available to provide significant parenting because she will not be able to be a full-time mother, full-time student and part-time worker. Third, the mediator establishes and enforces ground rules that encourage parties to attack problems rather than attacking each other.

Future-Focused Rather Than Past-Focused Attitudes

Family mediators are able to achieve remarkable success in a very short time because they focus primarily on the future, rather than on the past. Certainly some facts about the past are necessary to an understanding of the case and the issues presented. However, a future focus allows the couple to make progress because it frees them from trying to accomplish the almost impossible task of reaching agreement on what went wrong with the past or whose fault it was that caused the divorce. If important questions about why the marriage failed remains for one spouse, a referral to divorce therapy may be necessary where they can reach a conclusion about those questions.

The adversarial process of divorce requires attorneys to prove facts about the past in order to justify their positions concerning the case. An attorney may spend significant time in trial attempting to show that the husband had discouraged the wife from ever working and that he is at fault for her current lack of employment skills, or the attorney may show that the husband had very little contact with the children in the past because he was always working, and therefore he should not be awarded custody of the minor children.

To these past facts, the divorce mediator says, "So what?" The past cannot be changed and it is imperative that the couple learn new behaviors to make the new separate living arrangements work. By focusing on the future, the couple becomes less emotional about the pain and disappointments of the past, thereby reducing blaming and fault-finding communication patterns. Both benefit from this different attitude shift because the focus on the future also allows the couple to let go of the past and move forward in the emotional stages of the divorce process.

Rather than asking couples to decide who will have a higher level of ownership of the children based on who was a better or worse parent in the past, the couple is asked to develop agreements about the future care and exchange of the children so that each can be the good, loving parents they wish to be. Rather than asking them to determine amounts of child support based on who won custody of the children, the couple is asked to reach agreement on a fair method of sharing the costs of raising the children in the future. Instead of asking the couple to

agree on who is at fault for causing the wife to become
financially dependent and unable to earn an income, the
couple is asked to agree upon and implement a plan to
eventually enable the wife to become financially independent. Rather than asking them to divide their property
based upon who worked the most to accumulate the marital assets, the couple is asked to divide the property in a
manner that meets their standard of fairness and thereby
provides for the needs of each of them in the future.

Assertive, Not Passive, Aggressive or Defensive Attitudes

For the process theory of divorce mediation to be successful, mediators must develop skills that permit the
parties to become effective negotiators. This is most often
achieved through monitoring and guiding their discussions in such a way as to ensure that each is assertive
about what they want and need. Many couples enter mediation erroneously thinking that they have come to a place
where compromise is the underlying premise. Bolton (1979)
observes:

> Then, too, assertive behavior greatly reduces a per-
> son's fear and anxiety. Research has proven conclu-
> sively that learning to make assertive responses def-
> initely weakens the anxiety and tension previously
> experienced in specific situations. As the increas-
> ingly assertive person realized she can and will
> gain her needs and defend herself, she does not
> approach others with fears about being hurt or
> controlled.

One of the biggest pluses of assertive behavior is living one's own life. Your chances of getting what you want out of life improve greatly when you let others know what you want and stand up for your own rights and needs. Assertion . . . is results-oriented. . . . More of a person's needs will be satisfied by being consistently assertive than by submissive or aggressive behavior. (pp. 135–136)

The mediator reminds the couple that the definition of bargaining and negotiation is give and get. Couples are encouraged to see that a certain amount of trade-off and giving is essential to success in the process, but they must also be reminded that it will be necessary to learn how to clearly ask for what is needed to get their hopes for the future realized. In order to maintain a safe environment, the mediator must not allow either party to become aggressive and demanding, which causes the other spouse to become defensive and undermines the mediation process. The discussions should remain on a level that discourages verbal victimization. The mediator effectively accomplishes this by using many of the same skills developed and employed by therapists working with multiple parties in therapy sessions, such as reframing, clarification, and "I statements," to mention a few.

Encouraging an assertive attitude on the part of both parties also aids in the process of building boundaries and establishing improved self-esteem. Through referrals to financial planners, parenting classes, tax accountants, and therapists, the couple begins to learn and use tools that will help them live separate, independent lives. Independence, rather than codependency, now becomes the goal.

Positive Rather Than Negative Attitudes

For most couples, divorce is viewed as a tragic, stress-ful event, akin to a death in the family or, more accu-rately for some, the end of the world. In a competitive adversarial divorce process, attorneys tend to foster more negatives because the rules of the game are "Dog eat dog" and "If you don't fight hard now, you might get taken to the cleaners." Couples begin to fear the incredible losses they face: They might lose their children. They will cer-tainly lose money in the process of divorce and at the first meeting with their attorney, they are usually told the harsh realities of what they can and cannot expect to get in court.

In mediation, couples are told that they can mutually write the script for the future any way they wish, as long as that script is mutual and meets the needs of each. The mediator explains how they can achieve the goal for both of them to become good, loving parents in the future. They begin to see that they can achieve more through cooperation than through fighting. Hopefully, they learn that they are divorcing because the marriage relationship became a system of negative intimacies. Therefore, the task now becomes one of negotiating rules for building a positive plan for the future. Even for couples without children, the desire to end the marriage partnership with dignity is great and a skilled mediator will focus on pos-itives and minimize negatives. The definition of media-tion by Folberg and Taylor (1984) illustrates the process that stresses the commonalities:

Mediation tends to diffuse hostilities by promoting cooperation through a structured process. In contrast, litigation tends to focus hostilities and harden the disputant's anger into rigidly polarized positions. The adversarial process, with its dependence upon attorneys on behalf of the clients, tends to deny the parties the opportunity of taking control of their own situation and increases their dependence on outside authority. The self-esteem and sense of competence derived from the mediation process are important by-products that help to provide self-direction and lessen the need for participants to continue fighting (pp. 10–11).

The mediator employs several skills to intervene and accomplish this objective. Strange as it may seem, courtroom cross-examination skills can be very useful in this part of the process. The attorney cross-examines for the purpose of showing the witness in a negative act by exposing inconsistencies, evidence of bias, or other statements that help one side and hurt the other. In contrast, the mediator listens for the purpose of emphasizing a positive statement or act. That is, whenever something is said or done that evidences positive or common goals, it is quickly pointed out by the mediator and the parties are complimented.

The mediator is always trying to minimize the negatives or discuss negatives in a way that brings about positive change. A rule frequently mentioned by the mediator is, "Either of you may complain about something that you don't like, but any complaint or concern must also be followed by a positive, constructive statement about what can be done differently in the future to prevent the complaint from occurring again." This has the effect of encouraging the parties to create a positive plan for the future, rather than wallowing around in how dreadful the past has been.

3. NEGOTIATING METHODS

In addition to having good skills in managing communications and attitudes, the mediator employing the process theory of mediation must also have a strong understanding of negotiating methods. The actual bargaining process is the third building block of this conceptual framework and a mediator must be able to influence the parties in such a way as to help them let go of counterproductive bargaining methods and adopt new, more productive bargaining procedures. Much of what follows builds upon Fisher and Ury's significant yet simple book, *Getting to Yes* (1981). However, the concept of principled negotiations developed by Fisher and Ury must be specifically tailored to the unique process of terminating a family partnership involving intense emotions coupled with the business of raising children, paying bills and dividing property accumulated during the marriage.

Bargain About Interests Rather Than Positions

"Positional bargaining is always unwise" (Fisher & Ury, 1981, p. 5). A good example of positional bargaining is the custody battle. After a husband and wife file for divorce, they begin to think, "If I am not awarded custody of my children, I will lose them, and what's worse, I will wander around for the rest of my life being labeled a 'noncustodial visiting parent.'" Husband takes the position that in order to maintain his interests he must have custody. Wife takes the same position, only she wants exclusive or primary or physical custody, depending on the jurisdiction. What has just happened is that each has become convinced that the only position which maintains his or her interests and legal rights as a parent is to demand custody. Couples do not understand that once they take a position they have locked themselves into achieving their interest through one, and only one, mechanism. Unfortunately, the mechanism they have chosen allows for only one side's interest to be met, usually to the detriment of both.

Mediators employing the process theory of divorce mediation inform clients that they will first start bargaining about meeting their interests, rather than meeting their positions. This is accomplished by informing the couple that the use of the word custody tends to promote a positional stance and that when discussing children, we will focus on what you each want, not how you think you must achieve that want. This can be reinforced by pointing out that the only other place in our language that the word custody is used is in connection with prisoners. Furthermore, the only other place in our language that the word visitation is used is at the funeral parlor. Couples are asked to avoid negotiating about labels (positions) and rather are asked to negotiate about what they need. The mediator asks, "Do both of you agree that a goal of these discussions is to develop a plan which permits each of you to continue to be (or become) the good, loving parent you wish to be in the future, even though you will be living in two separate homes?"

By asking a completely different question, the focus of the mediation sessions thus becomes not *who* will have the children, but *when* each will have the children. Schedules, parenting styles, current needs of the children, and a host of other more important issues can then be discussed rather than wasting time on who was a better or worse parent in the past.

In cases where there are no children, the same type of question and process can be used. Often an issue arises around who will own the home. The mediator also addresses this issue from the aspect of interests and needs by asking, "What living arrangements do you each want in the future that will accommodate each of your needs?" This keeps them from locking horns over separate, often irreconcilable positions.

In contrast, the adversarial system, because it is competitive, requires divorcing couples to stake out extreme positions knowing that a court will never give them all they ask, but fearing that whatever they ask for will always be cut back in the negotiations. In addition, when a lawyer demands custody on behalf of the client, only one parent can achieve that goal of becoming a custodial parent. Yet, when a mediator suggests that each of them might be able to continue to be good, loving parents in the future, the couple has the chance to negotiate a resolution that allows each to achieve that end.

The ability to keep the parties from bottom-line positions is accomplished in other ways. Opening statements are prohibited and caucusing in separate rooms is seldom used because such methods only heighten the need to engage in positional bargaining methods. Such methods also diminish the trust level and tend to create a more adversarial atmosphere.

Attack Problems Rather Than Each Other

Negotiations are always more successful when concrete issues are discussed rather than when personal attacks against the other side occur. The mediator controls this by imposing and enforcing ground rules about safety. Whenever the actual negotiating method slips into personal attacks, successful outcomes are more difficult to achieve. Such discussions tend to contaminate the entire process by heightening negative emotions, increasing negative fears, and in general making it difficult to move from anger to positive implementation of plans that will help the couple unhook from the dreadful situation they find themselves in.

The most effective mediation technique used to implement this concept simply establishes the expectation that the couple will attack problems rather than each other. Knowing that the mediator is always ready to enforce this rule assures the couple that they will be working in a safe environment. It also reinforces the notion that fault will not be a primary factor in the determination of outcome because personal attacks are usually based upon something that was done or said in the past. When couples slip back into personal attacks, the mediator can learn a great deal from listening for the underlying concern that motivates the personal attack. By identifying the need expressed in the attack, the mediator can move the couple to a discussion about a range of options that will prevent that concern from occurring again.

Develop Fair Principles Each Can Accept, Rather Than Use a Law or Legal Precedent That Advances the Position of One Party Only

Fairness is not something that can be easily defined. In California, property in a divorce is divided equally. In New York, it is frequently divided unequally. This is because each has different concepts of what is fair when a husband and wife divorce.

The process theory of divorce mediation urges couples to search for and develop a standard of fairness they can both understand and accept. This means that it is not simply a matter of talking to a lawyer who will advise one of them about the prevailing law, which often changes like the wind depending on which lawyer is interpreting the law or which group in the legislature is writing the law.

A mediator employing the process theory must adopt several basic assumptions.

First and most important, the mediator must believe that people are basically fair or want to be fair and that almost all divorcing couples are capable of articulating what they think is fair. They may not be able to do this on their own, but given assistance from the mediator in the form of managing a searching and realistic discussion about fairness, the couple can construct a set of fairness principles. These principles are then compared with the outcome to test whether or not the principle of fairness has been met in the way the couple has decided various questions.

Second, the mediator must be willing to suggest some universal standards of fairness that appear to be acceptable to a wide range of divorcing couples. These can be posed in the form of questions such as:

1. *Do you both agree that it would be fair if a settlement were constructed that allowed each of you to continue to have a significant, loving relationship with the children?* (A yes answer to this question would eliminate a parenting schedule that prohibited the father from seeing the

children except on alternate Sunday afternoons from 1:00 p.m. to 2:30 p.m.)

2. *Do you both agree that a fair goal of these discussions is to reach an agreement about support that permits both of you to achieve some measure of economic security or stability, given the limited resources of the two of you and the different employment abilities each of you possesses?* (A yes answer by both to this question may result in an equal sharing of the income shortfall that exists or it may result in an extended period of spousal support by the husband to enable the wife to obtain further education or training to position herself better in the job market.)

3. *Do you both agree that you will divide your marital property in such a way that reflects your efforts at a marital partnership during the years you accumulated the assets?* (A yes answer to this question could result in an equal division of property or it could result in an unequal division of property in favor of one of them. But the choice is theirs to discuss, not for the state to impose upon them as so often happens in New York and some other states where a greater portion of the property assets may be awarded to the husband because he can show his income produced more of the accumulation of assets.)

In an adversarial divorce process, lawyers compete with each other to convince a judge (or bluff the other side) that their interpretation of the case laws (standards of fairness) is correct. However, the problem during recent years is that the law has become so complex, with so many competing interpretations, that it results in disagreement about what the standard of fairness really means and which standard of fairness should be applied. In an adversarial system, each side tries to interpret the principle of fairness in a way that advances or advocates one side's theory of the case. Little effort is expended in searching for a common standard that both sides can adopt and the choice is occasionally left to a judge who will try to strike a fair balance. More often than not, the judge chooses one side's interpretation of the standard to the detriment of the other side, based upon a fear of being overruled or based on a belief that even though the result may not be fair, the prevailing interpretation happens to favor one side on this particular day. All of this is very complex, cumbersome and quite costly.

Create Options That Benefit Each, Rather Than Options That Benefit One Party to the Detriment of the Other

Victory in the adversarial process usually determines one winner and one loser (or sometimes two losers). The combatants usually become locked into advocating options that can benefit only one side in the contest. An example of this is found in the area of nonmarital or separate property. In most states, when a gift or an inheritance is received by one of the parties during the marriage relationship, it is deemed to be separate property and not part of the assets to be divided upon divorce. However, should there be a dispute about whether it really meets the test of "separate property," a lengthy evidentiary trial may result in the option of including it or excluding it in the division of property. This is a win-lose option that could leave one side with no part of the asset. In the process of divorce mediation, parties are not limited to such narrow options. In one recent case in mediation, a couple became weary of the litigation process after each spending nearly $5,000.00 in preparing for trial on the issue of whether a 90-acre farm in the name of the husband truly met the test of separate property. Upon entering mediation, the couple were asked to think of other needs that had to be met rather than the mutually exclusive claim by the wife to half of the farm while the husband claimed she had no interest in the asset. When it became clear that the wife's greatest single need was to be secure in her retirement years, it was easier to solve the farm issue.

Ultimately, the couple constructed a settlement that called for the wife to release her adversarial claim to a half interest in the farm in exchange for the husband paying an additional $187.00 per month spousal support for 15 years. The extra $2000.00 per year was to be used by the wife for purchasing an Individual Retirement Account (IRA) each year and was deductible by the husband as Spousal Support. The total amount paid over time by the husband actually exceeded the value of the wife's claimed interest in the farm. However, with the tax deduction for spousal support, he found the option a reasonable price to pay for her release. Each spouse was able to feel satisfied about the outcome because both were asked to focus on their needs and then given assistance in brainstorming creatively about options that might meet those needs.

The process theory of divorce mediation asks parties to be creative and invent options that tend to meet the needs of each side. In the above example, the wife released her claim to the farm and the husband's need to transfer the property to the children was met. When the husband agreed to pay an extra $2,000.00 per year spousal support to be used for a retirement plan accumulated over 15 years, the wife's need for more security in her retirement years was met. The husband was able to deduct the extra spousal support and one could argue that the only loser was the IRS in that this option gave the wife about the same money as half the value of the farm, but reduced their taxes more than if the wife were to force a sale of the farm to collect her money.

In an adversarial process dominated by the rules of competitive play, the parties are in a sense locked into a game that requires each to say, "You're wrong and I'm right." In mediation, parties are urged to think that divorce is not as simple as applying the law of the state to a particular set of facts. It is very complex and in order to be successful both husband and wife must be committed to seeing that each is satisfied, not just one of them. It also requires them to engage in a process, or search for solutions; in that search, the answers begin to emerge.

The fourth building block of the process theory of divorce mediation looks at outcome goals. That is, when the parties begin negotiations, what are their goals?

4. OUTCOME GOALS

Both Will Be Winners Rather Than One Winning and the Other Losing

Because our laws require that divorce be treated like any other type of civil litigation, attorneys are required to act as zealous advocates in advancing their client's position. A mediator must act to advance both sides' interests or needs. Think of a divorce mediator and an attorney watching a football game together. The attorney might say: "If my team only had more money and more time to prepare, they might win." A mediator would respond by saying: "I think we should give both sides a football of their own, then they wouldn't have to fight over one football all day long." The attorney responds by exclaiming, "That would destroy the game!" to which the mediator says, "Exactly."

The game should be changed to allow the parties to fight hard together to overcome all types of common obstacles, such as the Internal Revenue Service, past debts hanging over both of their heads, and the extremely difficult task of raising children in two homes (when it is hard enough to raise children in one house with Mom and Dad together). When couples are reminded of the outcome goals during the course of the mediation discussions, such reminders provide the slight course changes so often needed when conflict causes them to stray into unproductive methods.

A Successful Divorce Is More Likely When the Couple Feels That the Needs of Each Have Been Met, Rather Than Each Feeling That Compromise Was the Result

All too often, couples enter mediation thinking that they will have to make major compromises to get a settlement. This is only true if they engage in positional bargaining. In the previous example of the 90-acre farm in dispute, each side held to a position and it was either win or lose on that position. Choosing some middle ground would certainly have felt like compromise to both. However, when the mediator focused on a general discussion of basic needs and tried to get the parties to work hard to meet those needs, it became easier to feel that both sides "won" when they finally chose a solution that met both sides' needs.

Compromise has a negative connotation in our competitive society. Indeed, if the mediator allows the couple to make opening statements, this has the effect of bargaining from extremes to compromising somewhere in the middle rather than encouraging them to go outside the positions into new, creative territory and explore new ideas and options. It is more productive to encourage the parties to first talk about their basic, underlying needs and then to creatively invent options that lead to solutions that met their needs to the greatest extent possible. The process theory of mediation requires a hard search by all three in the room for solutions that meet both sides' needs. The parties are positively influenced by hearing the outcome goals frequently repeated during the course of the mediation sessions.

Empowerment Rather Than Feelings of Being Overpowered

Frank Sander, a professor of law at Harvard University and a member of the American Bar Association's Dispute Resolution Committee, writes: "There is a world of difference between an adjudicated resolution and a resolution negotiated by the parties themselves" (1976, p. 122). When somebody else tells you what to do, it doesn't feel the same as if you decided to do it on your own. Therefore, this outcome goal urges the couple to create their own settlement because they are the best experts about what will be satisfactory. Indeed, if they don't accomplish the work themselves, somebody else will order a settlement imposed upon them. When someone else tells the couple what must be done, it often results in neither side feeling a sense of ownership for the settlement. This also creates a feeling of being overpowered which causes the loser to continue the battle after the legal divorce has been completed.

An Ongoing Relationship in Which There Is Some Dignity Rather Than Alienation of the Parties

Couples who obtain their divorce through adversarial methods and procedures often have battle scars and feel alienated. This is because an adversarial divorce process requires couples to engage in all of the competitive behaviors discussed above. It is extremely difficult to carry on a stable, trusting coparenting relationship having just completed a process that not only permits but requires all of the negative and counterproductive behaviors necessary to prevail in an adversarial process.

Couples who are encouraged by the mediator to follow the humane behaviors and negotiating methods of the mediation process not only achieve acceptable resolutions, but also avoid the battle scars and alienation that occur when the primary rule of the game is to show that the other spouse is defective as a parent, as a manager of money, or as a person.

CONCLUSION

Perhaps no other author had a greater effect on the early thinking of divorce mediators than Morton Deutsch. In his book, *The Resolution of Conflict, Constructive And Destructive Processes* (1973), Deutsch makes a compelling argument for the necessity of resolving disputes within a cooperative framework as opposed to a competitive framework. His early research on competitive and cooperative games established the theoretical framework for the need to have present many of the above discussed factors that are included in this conceptual framework of divorce mediation.

Fisher and Ury (1981) showed that you don't have to be a wimp in order to be cooperative. Indeed, their research at the Harvard Negotiation Project established the principle that nice guys can finish first. Their findings support the notion that the most ineffective negotiators are those who yell the loudest, stake out the most extreme positions, hold on the longest, and then cave in at the last moment to avoid impasse. Their book, *Getting to Yes*, establishes the framework for how couples can bargain and negotiate without reverting to hard-nosed, adversarial methods to achieve their goals.

Wallerstein and Kelly (1980) found that children of divorcing parents need not experience destructive and damaging effects provided their parents remain somewhat cooperative and avoid the tumultous and acrimonious battles of a bitterly litigated divorce. Joan Kelly is now in the process of completing research on several aspects of the divorce mediation process. In presenting her preliminary findings to the Academy of Family Mediators at its annual conference in July, 1986, she discussed the initial findings of comparing a control group of couples in the adversarial system and a similar group who completed mediation. Outcome satisfaction was higher in mediation than in litigation when women were asked to rate how they felt about the spousal support decision (Kelly, 1986). Likewise, Folberg and Taylor (1984) review the research concerning divorce mediation and conclude that the studies show significant rates of high satisfaction (pp. 11–13).

The conceptual framework of the process theory of mediation affords practitioners of family mediation a high degree of success because it is based upon traditional values of honesty, fairness, self-reliance, and hope for the future. Even though we have been conditioned to run to the courthouse to fight for our rights, the emergence of mediation need not be seen as an abrogation of those rights, but rather as a saner method of accomplishing a "successful" divorce.

2

Major Mediator Interventions

The role of the mediator is one that is often elusive and difficult to define with any specificity. The word "mediation" does not automatically create in people a cooperative approach to conflict resolution. That is, mediators are not magicians, but a mediator is expected to positively affect the conflict by doing something. What that something is has often been difficult to describe and analyze. Therefore, the following is a listing of specific mediator interventions that are essentially categories of activities in which mediators engage to promote cooperative behavior. It is important for mediators to think in terms of these categories because they provide a conceptual framework that is helpful in planning strategies for mediating each situation. The way to determine which interventions are appropriate is to first listen to what each person is saying and doing, and then to test the waters with various methods of controlling and influencing the process. Some interventions are used in every case. Others may not always be necessary.

PHYSICAL SETTING

The physical setting is one stage that can be manipulated by the mediator. This involves the arrangement of the table and chairs in the room, as well as the seating of the participants. It is usually wise to place the mediator about equidistant from the participants. If a mediator is too close to one of the participants, it can upset the desired balance and neutrality.

Beginning mediators also report that there is a drastic change in the tone and quality of the sessions when the mediator moves from behind a large imposing desk into a circle around a coffee table or some other work area. The idea is to create a setting where all participants are engaged in a joint task of solving certain problems. Compare the mediation room where the participants are all seated around a low coffee table to the physical setting of a court room with the judge on the highest level and the opposing parties squared off across a table ready to do battle with their advocates at their side.

EMOTIONAL SETTING

The emotional setting is another stage that must be controlled and molded by the mediator. Regardless of what types of mediation cases are being handled, it is always important to encourage a cooperative and mutual emotional framework. There should always be an initial consultation or orientation session related to the purpose of the mediation sessions. At the initial session, themes of mutuality and cooperativeness can be discussed and reinforced. In this orientation session, a simple statement comparing and contrasting the conflict resolution choices can also enhance the emotional setting. For example, the mediator may say to the participants: "The adversarial system takes the position that you can achieve gain for yourself only at the expense of the other person or other side. This is the wrong way of going about problem solving. Instead of your attacking each other, I will try to help the two of you attack the problem."

This kind of statement is a part of providing an orientation to the mediation process, as well as a way of shaping the emotional setting so that cooperative behavior will occur. Mediators expect that the problems can be solved by the parties and this assurance often relieves some of the emotional stress. The parties are expected to work on the solution and are encouraged each step of the way by the mediator. The atmosphere in the room is positive and hopeful. All of these attitudes add to the emotional setting.

PROCEDURAL SETTING

There are certain rules or procedures that mediators use to set a framework of cooperation. This is called management of the procedural setting. Many mediators operate within a set of written rules or guidelines. Others use an informal, unwritten set of rules. Whichever they use, all mediators should provide clients in conflict with a procedural framework. In fact, if the mediators do not provide such a procedural framework, the mediation sessions might proceed like an unstructured bull session and the neutral third party would function as a participant, not a mediator.

This procedural framework may consist of rules and procedures about time limits, fees, communication rules within the session, confidentiality, the selection and ordering or prioritizing of issues, and a host of other rules that relate to the mediator's control and management of the process. Each rule is tied to the overall goal of creating an environment that promotes cooperative behavior. The rule that there be confidentiality is tied to the concept that it is impossible to have people bargain and negotiate a settlement of their conflict if they have a fear that anything that is said in the sessions could later be used against them in court.

Mediators may decide to create all sorts of other rules, but each rule should be tied to a coherent concept of encouraging cooperative behavior. Some mediators have established rules that say you must speak only for yourself and you may not say what you believe the other person is thinking or feeling. Other mediators establish rules that permit them to intervene in the discussions to prevent verbal victimization. Whatever rules are used, they should be imposed only with restraint and then only when they advance the process of mutuality and cooperative decision making. In other words, the mediator should always be able to explain to the participants the reason for any rules adopted or imposed, since the participants must, in the final analysis, accept the imposition of the rules in order for them to be effective.

DEFINE THE ISSUES

It is often said that conflict is easier to resolve when people know what they are fighting about. In other words, it is very difficult to attain agreement on solutions if there is first disagreement about the exact nature of the argument. The mediator must often spend a majority of the early efforts in the mediation sessions in eliciting discussion and requesting agreement concerning what the dispute is about before proceeding with mediating solutions. During the years we have supervised beginning mediators, we have found that one of the most repeated mistakes which causes problems throughout the course of the mediation sessions is that the mediators forge ahead with the mediation before obtaining agreement about the conflict itself. Most conflicts are easier to manage if you direct your first efforts towards getting agreement on a definition of the problem or issues.

A clear example of how this can be a problem is found in the case of community groups in conflict with a school board over the closing of neighborhood schools. The conflict will be very difficult to resolve if the school board is willing to define the problem only as one of budget problems and funding shortages while the community is willing to define the problem only as one of community control of neighborhood schools. If both sides persist in approaching the problem from those two different perspectives without allowing that there is another way to define the problem of which schools to close, we can see that it will be very difficult for them to negotiate.

Another example of this crucial point can be found in the case of a wife who says, "I don't want him to see the children because he's a bad father." The mediation is already lost if the discussions center around whether or not one is a good or bad parent. That is an issue that can seldom be successfully mediated. It is possible, however, to mediate the issue of what exactly the father is doing that makes the mother conclude he is a bad parent. Once it is determined why the wife feels the husband is not doing a proper job of parenting, then it is possible to see if both can agree on certain improvements. However, in order to maintain balance, it is also necessary to ask the individual being put on the spot what items need improvement from the other side. If this approach is successful, the definition of this problem is shifted from "He is a bad parent" to "What specific things can be done by the two of you to make you better parents in the eyes of each other and your children?"

The mediator must strive to consistently state the problem in mutual terms. Solutions are easier to obtain when problems are stated in such a way that both sides share the burden of the discussions rather than each trying to defend against the fault-finding statements of the other side.

NARROW THE ISSUES

It has been said that the person who controls the definition of the issue controls the outcome.

Problems that are stated in broad, global terms are much more difficult to resolve than those problems that are narrowly defined. An example of this would be a parent who says to the mediator, "My son is impossible and incorrigible." First, to define the problem as that of incorrigibility of the child places everyone in a corner because it allows only one person to be responsible for causing the problem. When the problem is defined in a mutual fashion, it requires the understanding that more than one person is responsible, and therefore the effort towards a solution does not rest solely on the shoulders of the child.

Even if it were possible to state the problem of incorrigibility as a mutual problem (those who believe in a systems approach to the family would say that the entire family has a problem), the labeling of one person as incorrigible presents a difficult task for the mediator. It becomes necessary to narrow the issue so that it can be dealt with. What is the child doing that causes the parent to label him as incorrigible? There are many complex components to the term incorrigible, and mediators who are able to narrow the issues into smaller parts find that they have an easier time helping people resolve their conflict.

CONTROL THE DISCUSSION OF THE ISSUES

A mediator is essentially a manager of the process. As such, the mediator must make many decisions about whether or not the course of the negotiations is going in such a way as to be helpful to the resolution of the problems. One basic rule is that the mediator must make the mediation room a safe environment. The mediator must control the emotional outbursts, sharp statements, and other forms of blaming or nonproductive communication, so that nobody is victimized. A certain amount of "letting off steam" may be necessary and helpful, but a mediator must constantly monitor the people to see that everyone is protected. Beyond controlling this type of content, the rest of the mediator's management efforts become more subtle and harder to define.

First of all, mediators control the agenda and order of the various issues that have been agreed upon as open for discussion. People in conflict usually make progress toward resolution of their problems by taking small steps. To direct this, the mediator often prioritizes the issues from easier to more difficult. That is, the smaller, more easily managed issues are generally taken first.

A second way mediators manage the discussions is to keep people task-focused. Persons in conflict tend to wander around in their discussions, often getting side-tracked into areas that do not advance the course of the settlement. Perhaps more often, people simply don't have the ability to objectively listen to the negotiations and determine whether they are staying on task. Individuals participating in mediation may have so many feelings and emotions influencing their discussions that they will start to wander from the tasks.

The mediator can eliminate much of the bickering and static in the room by periodically reminding them to focus on the task when they appear to be straying into unproductive bickering. A useful intervention in the mediation room is the following: "I am going to ask that you stop arguing about who is responsible for this mess. I am sure that if I sat here for three days, I would never be able to sort out who was more guilty. But that is not my function. I am here to help you work out a resolution to your conflict. Now, could we get back to the issue of whether these income projections for next year are reasonable."

Try to think of the mediator as a traffic cop, directing the traffic flow of communication in such a way that it is orderly and proceeds from small agreements to larger agreements and on to finally fine tuning and balancing the entire package. Of course, one should not go over-board. If the mediator is too controlling, the people in conflict may begin to feel that the mediator is so involved in the discussions that any solution becomes the media-tor's solution. A balance must be struck. In fact, one of the most obvious indicators of a successful intervention is when the participants in conflict begin to get so in-volved in the search for solutions that the mediator can then take a less active approach to the discussions. Some mediators maintain that the sessions are not progressing well if the mediator has to do more talking than the par-ticipants.

Finally, by leaving resolution of the larger, more diffi-cult issues until last, the participants in the mediation session will have developed a stake in the successful completion of the process, because they have begun a history of agreeing on smaller, more easily determined issues. This is particularly true if the mediations continue over the course of several months.

HELP DEFINE INTERESTS AND NEEDS

Many people engaged in conflict, when given the op-portunity to state what they need in order to resolve the conflict, have a great deal of difficulty in formulating a statement of what they want. This is due to the fact that it is easier to complain about what is wrong than it is to state with specificity what will solve the problem. This would be even more the case where the definition of the conflict is also vague or undefined. (How can you say what you want in order to end the conflict if you do not understand the nature of the conflict?)

Mediators serve a very important function when they help people define their interests and needs. By focusing on each person's needs, the mediator reinforces the principle that a goal of mediation is to get each person's needs met. If mediators assume that most individuals are basically motivated by self interest, then an important strategy of the mediator is to see that each person's self interests are met by the arrangements that settle the conflict.

An interest or a need is different from a position. This is a distinction that will become more important later. The statement, "I will sell this house for $95,000.00 and not a penny less" is a positional statement. It reflects a need or interest that really says, "I have a need or desire to sell my house for the highest possible price I can obtain and I believe the highest possible price is $95,000.00."

Another positional statement that one hears is, "We absolutely must have $5,000.00 for the choir fund or the whole program will be wiped out." Such a statement reflects a need for financial levels that may or may not be possible or even necessary. The demand for $5,000.00 is a positional statement that states a solution. The need or want may be for new robes or different music or perhaps salary for a director. Indeed, it may be possible to get the needs met without the expenditure of exactly $5,000.00 and the mediator should go beyond the positional statement and concentrate on the underlying need. One cardinal rule that must always be followed is to focus on needs and interests *before* addressing solutions or positional statements. The reason is that needs and interests can be met in several ways, thereby giving the parties a wide range of options to choose from when negotiating solutions.

BARGAIN FROM INTERESTS, NOT POSITIONS

Positional statements or requested solutions can be met in only one way. If the mediation sessions revolve around a series of positional statements, the only room for negotiating is in the compromise that might be reached between two positional statements. However, if the mediator focuses on interests and needs, the eventual result of each person's needs being met is more likely to be achieved than the focus of one person's position prevailing over the other. This is what mediators mean by win-win solutions rather than win-lose solutions. It simply means that it is easier to obtain win-win solutions by focusing on interests and needs and limiting discussions about positions until needs have been clearly defined.

In fact, a positional statement is little more than a solution and few clients are able to propose solutions until there has been an opportunity to explore needs, interests, options, standards of fairness and creative solutions. After this type of work has been completed, each person's position can be explored. Given this way of ordering the steps of process of mediation, most family mediators discourage couples from making "opening statements," which is a traditional approach in the labor mediation format.

As Fisher and Ury (1981) so correctly point out in their book, the best negotiators are not those people who stake out the most extreme claims, yell the loudest, and cave in just at the last minute in order to avoid impasse. In fact, the best negotiators are those who try to make sure that the underlying needs and basic interests of each party to the negotiations are met. Where parties to a conflict have widely divergent positions, the only way to reach settlement is either through compromise or by one side winning and the other side losing.

HELP EACH REACH AGREEMENT ON THE FACTUAL BASIS FOR DECISION-MAKING

Regardless of the topic being mediated, another role of the mediator is intervention to assist the parties in agreeing on the facts. Most books written about decision-making for executives stress the need for obtaining accurate facts as one of the first steps in sound decision-making. This is no different in mediation. Just as it is important to have parties agree about the definition of the problem, it also important to agree upon the factual basis which underlies the decision-making process. Many court trials in the adversarial system consume extensive time and effort in presenting the facts to a neutral decision-maker. One of the key differences between the adversarial system and mediation is that facts become an important basis for future planning rather than for a determination of fault or guilt.

Much effort in mediation is spent managing the exchange of information concerning facts. It is important to realize that it may not be possible or even desirable to strive for total agreement between the parties on all factual issues raised. Since mediation is essentially forward-looking, be alert to the idea that some facts may be less important than future solutions. Many people in mediation think it is their task to convince the mediator of all the nasty facts that occurred in the past. Be prepared to distinguish between fault finding and necessary discussions about past facts. It is less useful to spend time on some past incident or disagreement. As mediators gain more experience, it becomes easier to determine which facts are essential for resolution of the issues and which facts are less important.

HELP DEFINE OBJECTIVE STANDARDS OF FAIRNESS

Problems are easier to solve if we can apply some standard in order to judge the outcome. An example of this is the divorcing couple who say, "We intend to divide all our marital property equally." A 50/50 division is a standard of fairness that, applied to outcome, allows for determining whether or not the division has been fairly achieved.

Another standard of fairness discussed and frequently agreed to by couples in divorce mediation is the statement: "We agree that our parenting arrangement should allow each of us to have significant contact so that the children see us as equal parents." However, some couples agree that it is better to have one primary parent. If both agree to this concept, they have adopted an objective standard that allows the outcome to be judged for fairness and quality. A skilled mediator will concentrate on managing the couple's discussions around this issue before seeking solutions. Experience will often show that if the couple is having difficulty agreeing on parenting arrangements, they have often missed the step of agreeing on objective standards to judge the outcome.

PROMOTE REALITY

Another function of the mediator is to provide a healthy dose of reality to the participants in the mediation process. Frequently, people involved in the conflict cannot see the forest because the trees are blocking their view. They may have unrealistic expectations about what they want or need, or they are unwilling to accept the fact that the financial data and budget projections do not permit any solution other than reducing their combined standard of living. It is important to help the people realize what is possible and what is not possible.

The following important word of caution is in order, however: When the mediator intervenes to promote reality, it is very important to do it in such a way that the parties do not feel that the mediator is taking sides or showing a bias in favor of one of the participants.

FIND MUTUAL OPTIONS FOR SOLUTIONS

The normal state of human affairs seems to be that it is easier to complain about something than to figure out a way to fix it. In mediation, people often need help in creating options that will meet the needs of all who are involved in the conflict. A general rule to keep in mind, however, is that it is always better if the solutions and options are generated from the participants rather than being suggested by the mediator. Creative mutual options are those that by their very nature give something to both sides. These mutual options should not be confused with compromise.

The best example of a mutual option in custody issues is the term joint custody. Conceptually, joint custody allows both parties to say that they have won custody of the children, if winning is important to them. At the very least, joint custody doesn't create a loser as nobody has really lost anything.

DRAFTING THE AGREEMENTS

Drafting the agreements made in mediation is an important function of the mediator. The mediator can help people in conflict find ways of expressing their solutions in a way that is clear, written in plain English, and stated in a manner that also records the reasons they decided to choose such solutions.

On those occasions when couples have contacted me years after their divorce has been entered, they have always referred to the mediation agreement rather than the legal decree of divorce. A well-drafted parenting agreement will be more useful to a couple than the custody paragraph in their divorce decree since many lawyers choose not to include all of the language of the mediated parenting agreement.

Parenting needs, goals and interests can be outlined in the mediation agreement, whereas this type of language is often inappropriate for the formal decree of dissolution. Care should be taken to help the couple realize that while written agreements are important, no document, no matter how carefully and completely it is drafted, can ever substitute for the ability of the parties to renegotiate future changes when necessary. The mediated parenting agreement should be viewed as a guide—a statement of goals and understandings—not as something that should be waved in the face of the other parent just before commencing contempt of court proceedings.

CONCLUSION

The above narrative is by no means an exhaustive listing of mediator interventions. Controlling time and the management of the audience effect are also categories of mediator interventions that may be viewed as separate and discrete types of interventions.

At a recent training seminar for mediators, the "expert" said to the group, "I can't really explain what one does as a mediator, but just watch me in this next role play and you will see what mediation is all about." Such statements perhaps typify the infant state of the art of conflict management. However, if the mediator can begin to see his/her activities as part of an overall conceptual framework of interventions, to be used not just because it seemed to be the thing to say at the time, but as part of a well-defined and intricate process, then we are nearing the goal of being able to teach others a more constructive approach to problem solving.

3

Dan and Linda:
A Typical Divorce
Mediation Case

FACTUAL BACKGROUND

The following case of Dan and Linda represents what I believe to be typical of the more than 500 divorce cases I have mediated since 1977. I selected this particular case because it has several elements that make it challenging. The couple had been married fifteen years and Roman Catholic religious values affected their decision to divorce, as well coloring the negotiation process. In addition, the case raises difficult support issues due to the fact that the husband earned $65,000.00 per year and the wife was unemployed. She had not worked outside the home since the marriage and had great difficulty viewing herself in a role other than homemaker and primary care-taker of the children. Another complicating factor was that the wife claimed she did not understand why her hus-band asked for the divorce. During their five-month sep-aration prior to entering mediation, Dan had very little contact with the two daughters, Marie, age 9, and Den-ise, age 13.

INTAKE PROCEDURE

At the first meeting, I provided Linda and Dan with a typical first hour "orientation session." This consists of accomplishing three objectives: first, I allow the three of us to interact so they can determine whether or not they feel comfortable with me as a neutral mediator; second, I give them detailed information about the goals and as-sumptions of the mediation process so that they might have some understanding of my ground rules and of what to expect should they decide to enter mediation with me as the mediator; third, I obtain information from them by explaining that if I know something about their conflict, I can then explain how I would go about helping them resolve their most disputed issues.

I view this first session as crucial in that it is less a diagnostic or intake session where the mediator gathers information and makes a diagnosis about their problems, than a marketing or sales meeting with the couple where I attempt to convince them to use the mediation process. Between the orientation session and the first working session, I ask them to complete a detailed six-page ques-tionnaire. Therefore, the first consultation does not in-volve taking a detailed family history, but is instead a discussion of their situation in more general terms. With

Linda and Dan, I asked enough basic questions to learn that they had been living apart for five months, had been separated for a short time three years ago and, through counseling efforts with their priest at that time, they had reconciled after Dan had been out of the house for five weeks.

At the first consultation, I attempted to learn from them their largest concern. One diagnostic question I always ask is, "If you could pick the most immediate issue, the most important unanswered question, what would it be?" For Linda, she stated that finances were most worrisome right now; for Dan, money was a problem, but he also indicated he was very concerned about not having much contact with his children since he moved out of the house.

At Linda and Dan's initial consultation, I also provided a picture of how I conduct mediation sessions. I indicated that I would always keep the mediation room a safe environment and would not allow cheap shots. They would each be required to speak for themselves and I showed them a copy of my Rules and Guidelines (see Appendix A) which ask them to adopt various written rules about confidentiality of the process and attendance at mediation sessions, as well as requiring them to not sell marital property or incur large debts without first obtaining the approval of the other, and to refrain from cancellation of any life insurance, health insurance or other benefits unless it is first discussed and agreed to in mediation. I asked them to each independently complete a detailed questionnaire about property, income, expenses and other financial information (see Appendix C). When Dan asked at this point why they couldn't fill out one questionnaire together, I explained my need to know who has the most (or least) knowledge about marital assets and marital finances.

At one point during the first consultation I asked both of them why they decided to come to my office to explore using mediation. Dan responded first by saying that he did not like attorneys, had once known a colleague at work who went through a bitter, contested divorce, and hoped that this might keep them from becoming enemies. Linda said she had talked to several attorneys immediately after Dan moved out of the house and one of them had suggested mediation as a possibility while another attorney had warned her in very strong terms not to consider mediation as it would not protect her "rights."

Although I did most of the talking at their first session, I learned that since the separation Dan had been sending Linda $450.00 every two weeks and paying the $495.00 per month mortgage payment on the house. Neither Dan nor Linda showed excessive emotions at any point during the first session, but I could sense the tension in the room at all times. When I asked about the children, Dan said that he had seen them only for short periods of time. Linda stated defensively, "He can see them any time he wants, I've never prevented him from being with them." At this point, I intervened by commenting about how there was really no need for Linda to defend herself, as Dan had not really accused her of withholding the children from him, but was saying that he felt bad about not seeing them more. Indeed, Dan helpfully pointed out that their 13-year-old had really grown away from him and he wasn't quite sure what could be done about it.

I then asked Linda to describe her view of how the children were accepting the separation. I purposely ask this form of question to move the discussion away from putting Linda in a position where she feels she must defend herself. I concluded this discussion by pointing out the importance of establishing schedules of exchanges and suggested that they buy a copy of the book *Mom's House, Dad's House* (Ricci, 1980).

We then covered some final points by discussing fees and meeting with the children. I asked them a closing question, "Now, based upon what I have described, does this sound like something both of you wish to do?" Dan responded first by saying he thought they should schedule a first working session. Linda said she thought they should wait. Based upon what I had observed during the previous 45 minutes, I took a risk and asked whether she was concerned about the fact that Dan had refused to attend marriage counseling sessions with her and whether she was really hoping that something would happen to change his mind about the relationship. She responded by saying that the children would be starting their first day of school in two weeks and she had much to do to get them ready. She suggested that a first working session be scheduled after the children started school. I was again reminded of something that is very difficult to learn: it is best not to assume anything unless you first inquire about your assumption.

We scheduled a first working session for the week after their two children began school and I sent them away with questionnaires to complete along with copies of the Rules, a copy of the Agreement to Begin Mediation form (see Appendix B) and suggestions about where they could obtain Ricci's book. In addition to impressing them with the importance of completing the questionnaire by the first session, I also asked them to be thinking about how they will share the fees. Dan responded by saying that he would pay them. I asked them to think about a way they could handle the fees so that both felt they were sharing in the cost of mediation.

PROCESS USED TO ANALYZE CASE

My case file shows about three lines of notes to myself written a few minutes after they left. It reminded me to explore marriage counseling again and further says, "He wants the divorce, she doesn't but is resigned to the idea that if it has to happen, she would rather be in mediation." At this point, after one hour with Linda and Dan, I really don't feel I have enough information to analyze the case. Indeed, I have come to believe that it is useless and even detrimental to my function as a mediator to begin "analyzing" the case after only a one-hour meeting with the couple. Such a view is quite different from the approach a therapist or lawyer would take.

Before becoming a mediator, when I represented one client as an attorney in divorce cases, I would immediately analyze new cases from the point of view of trial strategy, and my file notes contained numerous speculations about what the outcome might be if we went to trial on such a case. As a mediator, I soon found out that taking on the role of an oddsmaker about the outcome in court was not helpful. Although I am ultimately concerned that couples have some notion of how courts usually rule in typical dissolution cases, I must not fall into the trap of telling them what I think the court's ruling would be under the facts of their case and then say, "Now, I think you should construct a settlement that is similar to what our courts would do." Such an analysis is commonly made by many beginning divorce mediators with legal backgrounds and I try as much as possible to refrain from speculating about the "proper" or desired outcome that would be obtained in court.

Similarly I find it of little use to engage in an analysis

of the case as my therapist friends do after a first interview. That is, I do not think it is proper for a mediator to speculate about who is more ready for the mediation process or whether or not one of them has yet to accept the divorce. I find that, although such information may be helpful in my management of their negotiations, after only one session I am never able to make correct assumptions about such issues of "emotional readiness" or diagnostic determinations about what roadblocks might later materialize.

Rather, I analyze each case from the following point of view: 1) Which of the three main divorce mediation issues (parenting, support, property division) should I have them first discuss; 2) Do they understand the goals and assumptions of the mediation process; and 3) If I select one of three major issues to discuss at the first session, which one will have the greatest chance of allowing them to leave the first working session feeling they have achieved substantial progress towards making important agreements. In the case of Dan and Linda, I decided to start with the custody/parenting issues because even though they both said finances were an important issue, they also agreed that the children were experiencing some adjustment difficulties and Dan was concerned that he had not seen the children very much during the separation period (approximately five months).

CONCEPTUAL FRAMEWORK USED TO MEDIATE CASE

To be successful, a mediator should operate from some theoretical framework. With every case, I follow a structured approach that involves the following steps for each major issue. Although these steps are not rigid in sequence, they essentially occur in the following order:

1. **Orientation** or consultation and obtaining commitment to mediation as a process that will be used to resolve divorce issues.
2. **Gathering, displaying and organizing the facts:** This must be done in such a way as to be understandable for the couple. Good decisions must be based upon good facts.
3. **Defining issues:** Participants in the mediation process need to know what the conflict is about. For example, I will make it easier for them by suggesting that the dispute is not an issue of who was a better or worse parent in the past, thereby establishing who will have a higher or lower level of ownership of the children which results in one of them being labeled a noncustodial visiting parent for life. Rather the issue is: What future parenting arrangements can be agreed to so that each of you can be the good, loving parents you wish to be even though you are living in two separate places?
4. **Discussing fairness:** Agreement on the principles of fairness is an essential step in moving the couple towards agreement. Do they believe that an equal division of property is fair or do they believe that an unequal division of property, giving the wife more assets, balances the fact that she dropped out of school to help pay for the husband completing his M.B.A.? Is exactly equal time sharing of the children a standard of fairness that meets the test of being good, loving parents or is it possible that an unequal time-sharing arrangement will still allow them to meet their mutual parenting goals?

5. **Defining needs:** Regardless of what everyone else says about the divorce process, if couples can state what their needs are, and then get those needs met, the case will settle. All couples facing a dissolution of their marriage have three basic needs: (1) some plan for seeing financial security (or the hope of such security) in the future; (2) a method of continuing to be good, loving parents; and (3) a process of dividing property that results in meeting their definition of fairness.

6. **Creating mutual options that meet each spouse's needs:** There is no single way to solve a problem. Brainstorming about solutions allows people to see that there is more than one way to reach resolution and the goal is to arrive at a settlement option or series of settlement options that gets the primary needs of both met.

7. **Selecting the options that meet most of the needs of each:** This is the process of bargaining and negotiation—the give and take of the discussions that allows both husband and wife to see that when each is willing to cooperate in getting the needs of the other met, one's own needs will then begin to be met.

In addition to following these procedural steps, I also operate from a conceptual framework that says: Mediators should intervene only when it is necessary to move the couple from a competitive bargaining process to a cooperative process. That is, I attempt to encourage the factors necessary for mutual problem solving rather than adversarial problem solving. I attempt to influence communication and attitudes in such a way that the environment for cooperative problem solving is created.

Communication is the tool for exchanging information. I encourage open and honest communication by assuring them that the rules prohibit each from ever using statements made in mediation against the other in court. I ask for open and honest communication by making the room a safe environment and by openly addressing instances of what appear to be guarded or secretive statements. I rarely caucus individually with either spouse as this creates mistrust and suspicion.

I attempt to discourage coercive statements by listening for any type of communication that contains a threat or an if-then statement. I ask them to speak in a persuasive manner rather than a threatening manner. After all, a threat is merely a statement about one's fear that a basic need will not be met by the other except through threats.

I ask that the couple communicate without blaming or fault-finding statements. Such communication is the focus of the adversarial system and I will quickly intervene when it is apparent that the discussions center around establishing whether one was at fault for something in the past. I will allow them to complain, but will also ask that they follow their complaints with a positive constructive statement about what will solve the concern in the future.

Another part of my conceptual approach is to influence attitudes. I believe that mutual agreements can be obtained when attitudes shift from mistrust to trust. This is accomplished primarily through the technique of continually trying to achieve small agreements that have a high likelihood of successful completion and adherence. I also want the couple to realize a mutual attitude rather than an individualistic attitude. I accomplish this by teaching them about their connectedness and reminding them that they are in the soup together.

Perhaps the most powerful tool for achieving a mutual attitude is for the mediator to redefine the common divorce issues in a new way. Custody issues are not wars over control of the children, but rather important discussions about future parenting arrangements. The issue of child support is not seen as how much money the husband should pay to the wife for support of the children in her control, but rather a discussion about how each of them will share in the cost of raising the children. Alimony is not an issue of trying to stick the husband for as much as can be obtained, nor a process of squeezing the wife economically, but rather a discussion of what mutually agreed-to plan will be implemented to eventually eliminate the dependency of the wife.

Perhaps the most powerful tool in the mediator's entire approach is the constant focus on the future rather than on the past. By constantly managing the discussions in such a way that emphasizes the future and de-emphasizes the past, the environment for good decision-making is created. In the actual mediation session with Linda and Dan, some aspects of this theoretical approach and how it affects their decision-making are evident.

CRITICAL ISSUES PRESENTED

The first working session was scheduled for two hours. I opened the meeting by engaging in small talk about how the first day of school went for their children, and I asked them for their completed questionnaires. I had copies made for each of us. I explained that although I knew finances were an important issue, it appeared to me that they were also concerned about Dan's contact with the children and I asked if it was acceptable to them if we started discussing children's issues and then we would move to the financial concerns of each. They agreed to begin with children's issues.

My first question was, "What exchange agreements concerning the children have you been following during the past five months?" Linda said they have not really followed a schedule and Dan usually calls when he wants to see the children. Dan said there have been several occasions where he has called from work on Friday afternoon to see the children on the weekend and the older daughter has already made plans for the weekend. Linda commented on how it is difficult to force the children to see him as they have their own lives to live and they are both involved in school and church activities. I asked Linda if she felt it would be important for the children to see more of Dan. She readily agreed. I then engaged them in a discussion of my observation that most couples benefit from having a definite exchange schedule so that every family member will have certainty about the parenting exchange. A schedule seems to improve the separation process because it creates definite expectations for each family member.

Both commented on how it appeared that the children were reluctant to spend time with Dan. I then observed that such reluctance is not uncommon in the early stages of separation and divorce for two possible reasons: First, the children might not know that Mom and Dad expect them to spend some time with their father who is out of the house, and second, if the parents persist in asking children if they wish to spend some time with Dad on a given weekend, the parents may be putting the children in a situation where they are forced to express a choice—and children do not wish to express a preference because if they show a desire to be with Dad on the weekend, they fear they may be disappointing Mom. If they say to Dad that they would rather stay with Mom this weekend, they fear Dad will be disappointed. By not having a schedule, parents are putting the children in a box from which they can escape only by stepping up their activities with friends so as to avoid making a choice between either parent.

At this point, I moved to the flip chart and drew a large square with 28 blank boxes representing the seven days of the week for a four-week period. I asked each what schedule seems to be appropriate for each of them. I reminded them that at this point in their separation, they are novices at the art of separate parenting and it might be a good idea for them to consider this schedule as the beginning of an experimental period during which time they try to learn what specific schedule will serve their family best.

After about 20 minutes of exchanges among the three of us, the schedule (on p. 61) emerged.

They were both unsure about how Marie would react to a full weekend in Dan's apartment as she has never stayed overnight for a complete weekend. I suggested that they may wish to have a family meeting with the two children to explain the new exchange schedule. Both agreed that it might be a good idea, but then Linda said Marie was more concerned about Dad's new "girlfriend". In a calm manner, I asked Dan if he knew what Linda was talking about. He said this was the first he had heard of such a concern. Linda then said that the two girls also

M = Mom   D = Dad

	Mon	Tue	Wed	Thu	Fri	Sat	Sun
Week 1	M	M	M/D	M	M/D	D	D/M
Week 2	M	M	M/D	M	M	M	M
Week 3	M	M	M/D	M	M/D	D	D/M
Week 4	M	M	M/D	M	M	M	M

can't understand why Dad has left the family for another woman.

Resorting to my conceptual theory of mediation that says people need agreements not therapy, I asked Linda if she wanted a written temporary agreement that states Dan will not have his girlfriend stay with him when the children are present. Linda said nothing and I looked at Dan. He said that he does not live with another woman and that such an agreement was unnecessary. After a bit more prodding of each, both agreed that such an agreement was acceptable. I decided to leave this issue for a later point in the mediation discussions and proceeded to the finances.

I introduced the financial discussion by recalling that both were concerned about money. I complimented them on the fact that during the separation they had been able to agree upon an exchange of money on a temporary basis. Linda said there had been several recent occasions where the $1,000.00-per-month payment had not been enough and she had asked Dan for additional money. She was very concerned that he had turned down her requests twice, saying he couldn't afford to pay any more than he already was.

Using the flip chart as a display device, I asked each to get their questionnaires out and turn to the budget section. As we started to list each of their budgets on a single page of flip chart paper, I noticed that the two hours were almost up. I decided to end the session by complimenting them on their agreements reached concerning the children and asked a few remaining questions: When would the every other weekend schedule begin? Did they each have enough money to make it another week before becoming clear on a new financial arrangement? Would there be any need for either to incur new debts on the existing charge accounts? When should we meet again?

We scheduled the second working session for the following week. When they arrived, I moved quickly to the flip chart where we had started listing their expenses the previous week. After about one hour of work, the budget, which is found on pp. 64–65, emerged.

After completing this budget chart, I asked them if they felt the expense needs were reasonable for each. Dan spoke first and said he thought $200.00 per month for the children's clothing budget was high. Other than that category, both felt that the expense statements were not out of line for either. I then asked them what these numbers meant to them. Linda said it was clear to her there was no way they could make it living apart and she further pointed out that although Dan's budget was slightly less than her's, there are three of them and one of him. I did draw Linda's attention to the fact that we have created a third column for the children's expenses in order to deal with that issue separately.

As the discussion began to deteriorate around Linda's statement that if Dan were to move back home, they would not have to face any of these problems, Dan emphatically stated that she knew that was not possible. I chose to ignore the real issue of Linda still not accepting the divorce because this was the first time she had raised the issue since the orientation session and the discussions had not been angry until this point. I pursued my goal of injecting a bit of reality by reminding her that I knew she did not want to be sitting here, but she had stated the first time we met that if the divorce had to occur, she would rather be in mediation. At that point I asked each of them to take a five-minute break before continuing.

When we resumed, I focused back on the task. I observed that there are four choices when facing a shortfall. They can try to cut expenses. They can try to increase income. They can temporarily borrow from assets, or they can begin to use tax planning principles to reduce their taxes and therefore have more income to meet extra needs. I also suggested that some couples choose the principle of equal belt tightening to meet a shortfall if they find they cannot cut expenses any further and there is no way to immediately increase incomes.

I then proceeded to demonstrate the concept of equal belt tightening by using the flip chart.

Linda needs $1,776.00 plus $633.00 to meet her expenses and the children's expenses. Dan needs $1,626.00 plus $125.00 to meet his own expenses and the children's when they are with him. Dan earns $3,074.00 and Linda earns $300.00 a month. If Dan meets all of Linda's needs by transferring $2,109.00 per month to her, she will have her entire budget needs met, but he will have only $965.00

MONTHLY BUDGETS

Item	Linda	Dan	Children Pd. by Linda/Dan
Housing PITI (Principal, Interest, Taxes, Insurance)	495.00	525.00 (rent)	
Insurance	-0-	10.00	
Maintenance	25.00	-0-	
Replacement of H.H. Items	25.00	10.00	
Food, H.H. Supplies, Lunches	325.00	250.00	
Clothing	75.00	50.00	50.00/
Medical Insurance	through Dan	through work	200.00/
Uncovered Medical	5.00	-0-	through Dan 15.00/
Dental Insurance	-0-	through work	through Dan
Uncovered Dental	10.00	8.00	/35.00/
Medicine/Drugs	10.00	10.00	28.00/
Car Payments	145.00	225.00	
Gas and Oil	100.00	90.00	
Repairs/Maintenance	40.00	45.00	
License	9.00	8.00	
Auto Insurance	35.00	35.00	
Recreation	30.00	60.00	70.00/40.00
Life Insurance	28.00	-0-	
Electricity	55.00	20.00	

Gas/Heat	73.00	-0-	
Phone	45.00	25.00	
Water	12.00	-0-	
Garbage Removal	12.00	-0-	
Yard Maintenance/Snow Removal	12.00	-0-	
Drugstore Items	10.00	10.00	10.00/
Reading Materials	10.00	10.00	
Haircare	5.00	10.00	5.00/
Gifts	100.00	50.00	
Flagship Athletic Club		65.00	
Cleaning/Laundry	5.00	30.00	
Children's Misc. (Dance, Sports, etc.)			175.00/
Children's Allowances			50.00/50.00
Vacations	50.00	50.00	
Charities/Church	30.00	30.00	
Sitting Costs for Marie			30.00/
Totals:	$1,776.00	$1,626.00	$633.00/125.00

Total Monthly Combined Expenses . . $4,160.00

Total Monthly Combined Incomes . . . $3,374.00   (Linda earns $300.00/mo. as part-time secretary at church)

Shortfall . . . . $ 786.00

to meet needs of $1,751.00. The entire shortfall becomes his problem because he is $786.00 short. However, if he has all of his budget needs met, Linda will then be $786.00 short. (At this point, Dan said that he could now see it was necessary to increase the amount of money he had been paying her. Linda then asked what amount would represent each of them sharing the shortfall equally.)

I calculated the following numbers of the flip chart:

If Dan pays Linda .. $1,776.00
And Linda earns $300.00
She has $2,076.00
to meet needs for herself and
the children of $2,409.00
Linda's shortfall $333.00
And Dan earns $3,074.00
If Dan pays Linda .. $1,776.00
He is left with $1,298.00
to meet needs for himself and
the children of $1,751.00
Dan's shortfall........ $453.00

Linda said that since she has already purchased most of the clothing for the start of school, she felt the above arrangement would be an improvement and she probably wouldn't have to purchase any more clothes for a time. I pointed out that during the separation Dan has been paying Linda $900.00 per month and paying the $495.00 mortgage payment for a total of $1,395.00 per month. He has now agreed to increase his payments to Linda by $381.00 per month. Additionally, since Dan's net income is $3,074.00, a payment of $1,776.00 per month represents approximately 58% of his monthly net income. They agreed to this new arrangement and I asked them to try it for a few months to see if it would work. The two-hour session went 10 minutes extra and we concluded by setting the next working session for two weeks from that day.

At this point in the process, I have emphasized the principle that each should have the unrestricted right to state their needs by completing the budget without making negative comments about the expense needs choices of the other. I have explicitly stated that in order to arrive at a fair support arrangement, they must be able to see how each will spend their money and I have introduced a discussion about principles of fairness. I have also asked them to create some financial boundaries by being responsible for paying the expenses listed in their own columns. This particular couple decided to choose the concept of equal belt tightening and agreed to share the budget shortfalls equally. I have kept them from engaging in unproductive discussions by structuring the process so that they were kept so busy that they didn't have time to get into arguments. I have also brought them to the point of reaching a temporary agreement about parenting schedules and support in the span of two working sessions.

I asked Linda what her thinking has been about the possibility of increasing income after, at the end of the second session, Dan had blurted out that all of this would be a lot easier if Linda would just get out and look for a job instead of wasting her time as a part-time secretary at the church. I assigned Linda the task of thinking about a career plan for increasing her income and I asked Dan to obtain detailed information about his pension plan from his employer.

ROADBLOCKS IN THE WAY OF SETTLEMENT

The remaining three sessions were hard work, but progressed well except for several flash points.

Dan stated at the beginning of the third session that several friends at work have told him he is paying too much support to Linda.

I responded by initiating a discussion about what mediators call the "audience effect." I asked him if he felt he was paying too much support and he said he didn't really know. I reminded both of them that this was *their* divorce and *their* settlement negotiations. Indeed, he could find many attorneys in town who would tell him he was paying too much and I was sure that Linda could also find attorneys who would say he is not paying enough and if they were to take over the case, they could get her more money. I then said to Dan, "Are you asking that the temporary support payment be decreased?" No, Dan wasn't asking for that. He was again leading into his recurring theme of hoping that Linda would find work and contribute to the income needs of both. (This issue was settled at the last session.)

They agreed that the property division would be approximately equal and that they would divide the house. For now, Linda has the right to reside in the house until Marie reaches age 18. At that time the house would be sold and the net proceeds divided equally. However, when I asked them about including other contingencies that would require a sale of the house earlier than 10 years from now, they had a major disagreement about whether the house should be sold if Linda remarried.

I feared this would become a major issue after hearing Linda claim that if Dan were to remarry, the agreement doesn't require him to sell anything. Indeed, this issue became quite a problem because Dan had made a first visit to his attorney before the last session and was informed that judges routinely require a sale of the house upon the wife's remarriage. Moreover, his attorney also stressed that he should negotiate a clause that also required a sale of the house "upon the wife's cohabitation with another male individual not her spouse for a period of more that 90 days continuously." Linda objected loudly. I was quietly pleased that Linda was beginning to be a bit tougher in her negotiations because there had been many situations where she seemed to be content to let me find solutions.

After they expressed themselves in often heated terms about this issue for three or four minutes, I calmly observed that this is frequently a source of disagreement for couples. Indeed, with the two of them, it is an issue I would have expected to be a problem given the history of events surrounding the separation. I said that most couples who have trouble with this issue solve it by including a clause in their settlement agreement which says: "Should the person in possession of the house under a fractional lien arrangement remarry, rent to another adult or take on a roommate during the period of shared ownership, both agree to return to mediation and discuss whether or not the lien should be satisfied prior to the youngest child reaching age 18. They will consider the financial circumstances at the time of the event that requires a return to mediation and they will take into account the needs of the minor child or children remaining at home."

I explained that this simply means that it is often possible to be rigid on such important issues and the passage of time may allow both to be in circumstances that make this issue easier to resolve. I also observed that perhaps this was primarily a symbolic issue for both of them. I asked them to think about such language and review it with their attorneys. Both quickly said that they could not afford to spend a great deal of time with their attorneys who had already started billing them for each phone call and they would rather agree to such a clause.

At one point during the fourth working session, I was trying to pull together some of the remaining issues and I found that they had a major disagreement about the label "physical custody".

They were both in agreement that the Decree of Dissolution should contain a clause calling for joint legal custody, but Linda had been informed by her attorney that she should not agree to joint physical custody. When I asked her what she understood by her attorney's admonition that she be designated the physical custodian, she said that she has always been the primary parent and even though he wanted total joint custody, it was just not acceptable to her. I asked them a few more questions and then agreed with her that her attorney was absolutely correct—that if the two of them were to have major disagreements in the future about the children, or if one of them wanted to move out of state and take the children, the person who has been designated the "physical custodian" is in a better position to prevail in court. However, these labels become important only in the event the two of them end up in court in the future around a parenting disagreement.

I suggested that one thing other couples have done to eliminate the concern over labels is to include an arbitration clause that takes future disagreements away from the court and thus eliminates the whole concern over who has a higher or lower burden of proof in future court hearings. I went over a sample clause that calls for mandatory return to mediation and then binding arbitration by a panel of three mental health experts in the event of a future parenting dispute. After letting them read the sample language of the arbitration clause, I observed: "I think that the three mental health professionals will not really understand the legal significance of the label 'physical custody,' but be more interested in hearing from the two of you and your children and then deciding on a fair way to resolve the dispute." This intervention process resolved the dispute when Linda said she would agree to joint legal and joint physical custody upon inclusion of the binding arbitration clause in the Decree.

Perhaps the most difficult critical issue that surfaced was the discussions around Linda's plan for her own economic future.

Dan was anxious to end his spousal support obligations and Linda wanted some time to consider her career options. I bought time for both of them by referring them to a neutral tax expert for analysis and discussion of the tax effect of spousal support and child support. While the accountant was preparing several different options for the best mix between child support and spousal support, I asked Linda to meet with an employment specialist at a local Women's Resource Center. Indeed, Dan was more than willing to agree to assist in paying for such an interview. Linda had on several occasions expressed a desire to finish her nursing degree which was interrupted by their marriage.

At the last session, Linda returned with detailed information about the costs and time involved in completing three years of college level nursing courses to enter a specialty as a surgical nurse. She said she was told that she could expect to earn between $16,000.00 and $19,000.00 per year upon graduation and the tuition would be approximately $4,000.00 per year.

I expected Dan to be finally pleased with Linda's movement on her career plans, but Dan was way ahead of me. He was wondering if he would get stuck paying for the tuition. He didn't state it in the form of a question, but rather winced when I asked them to discuss the implications of Linda returning to school as a full-time student.

Dan stated that she would be able to afford the tuition and books from her one half share of the $18,000.00 money market account they planned to divide equally. Linda felt that Dan should pay for her tuition as she had dropped out of nurse's training in the first year of their marriage to help Dan obtain his M.B.A. degree. Linda then said to me, "You're a lawyer, can I ask you a legal question?" My standard response is that there are no legal questions, only questions. She wondered if she had a right to a share of his M.B.A. degree. I replied, "Why don't you ask Dan instead of me, since he is the one with the degree?"

At this point, the room again started to heat up and I intervened with a comment about how several courts, particularly New York State Courts, had ruled that a wife had an ownership interest in the husband's medical degree. I gave them my own opinion that it is probably easier to see the husband's degree as something that allows him to earn an income permitting him to pay spousal support. That is, rather than treating the degree as a property asset, view it as another aspect of the spousal support decision.

At this point their discussions degenerated into an exchange of opinions about who had worked the hardest during the marriage. Dan said that he had always encouraged Linda to work outside the home and she was rather more content. . . . At this point I forcefully interrupted their discussions and said, "I'm quite sure that if I sat here for the next three hours and listened to both of you, I would never be able to figure out all the facts exactly the way it happened. In fact, you didn't hire me to listen to the two of you present evidence about why Linda is now dependent upon the marriage for support. I'm sure that each of you would have made very different choices during the last 15 years had you known you would be sitting in my office today." For a moment, that settled them down.

I pointed out, "Linda, you have said that you hate the thought of getting money from a man who has left you. Both of you desire to end the dependency as soon as possible. Let's figure out a way to accomplish that goal." For the next 45 minutes, we explored a range of options and finally decided that there would be an unequal division of property, with some of the money market account being designated for tuition. They finally agreed to an equal division of all property except that Linda would receive $14,000.00 of the money market account and Dan would receive $4,000.00. Dan also agreed to continue existing support payments until Linda entered school full time at the beginning of the winter quarter. Because she would no longer be able to work part time at the church, he would raise the support payments by $300.00 a month which he planned to fund from an anticipated raise and a yearly bonus that had averaged between four and six thousand per year. The following Memorandum of

Agreement was dictated and sent to each of them, with an extra copy for their attorneys.

MEMORANDUM OF AGREEMENT

Linda and Dan (deleted) have made a decision to live separately and seek a dissolution of their marriage relationship. As a result of that decision, both have agreed to enter into mediation conducted by Family Mediation Services for the purpose of settling all issues which might otherwise be the subject of contested litigation. Prior to entering mediation, they signed an agreement with each other and with Family Mediation Services to be fair and equitable throughout the mediation process.

They understand that neither Family Mediation Services nor the mediator legally represents either or both of them. Both agree to retain attorneys of their own choice to legally represent them and to provide each of them with an independent judgment about the decisions reached in mediation.

Mediation was conducted by Stephen K. Erickson for Family Mediation Services. The following represents their intended decisions reached in mediation after careful review of all facts and options. Both have made a full disclosure to each other of the full nature and extent of their assets, and they wish their attorneys to incorporate the following into a legally binding settlement agreement.

Custody (Parenting Agreements)

Dan and Linda have two minor children of the marriage relationship: Denise Elizabeth, born 5-2-73 (age 13), Marie Kay, born 10-7-77 (age 9).

Dan and Linda have agreed to share joint legal custody and joint physical custody of the minor children. They have chosen this parenting arrangement as a way of sharing joint decision-making in the future regarding the children.

They understand that joint legal custody means that they will continue to cooperate in making decisions regarding education, medical treatment, religious training, and other important parenting decisions. Should they have any disagreements concerning parenting of the children, they agree to first try to resolve such differences between themselves, and to return to mediation if they are unsuccessful in resolving any issues or problems.

They also agree that joint legal custody means that each of them will continue to have equal access to all medical, educational and other important records of the children.

They agree that they will also share joint physical custody of the two minor children. They understand that this means each of them will have equal voice in the scheduling of exchanges, as well as in the physical living arrangements of the children.

They have agreed to a schedule of exchanges that calls for the children to be primarily with Linda and to spend time with Dan as follows:

M = Mom   D = Dad

	Mon	Tue	Wed	Thu	Fri	Sat	Sun
Week 1	M	M	M/D	M	M/D	D	D/M
Week 2	M	M	M/D	M	M	M	M
Week 3	M	M	M/D	M	M/D	D	D/M
Week 4	M	M	M/D	M	M	M	M

Binding Arbitration

Should they have disagreements in the future about any aspect of their parenting agreement, they will first meet and attempt to resolve such disagreements on their own. In the event that is not possible, either Dan or Linda has the right to request a return to mediation. After making a good faith effort to resolve the parenting dispute in mediation, if they are still at an impasse, they agree to submit the dispute to binding arbitration. The arbitration hearing will be governed by the Minnesota Arbitration Act and the Rules of Arbitration as established by Family Mediation Services, Inc. They agree that the arbitrators shall consist of a panel of three mental health experts chosen from a list maintained by Family Mediation Services. The cost of mediation as well as the cost of arbitration shall be shared on a pro-rata basis according to each of their gross incomes at the time of commencement of either process. They understand that by agreeing to binding arbitration of all future parenting disputes, they waive their right to have the dispute heard by a District Court judge and they agree to be bound by the ruling of the arbitrator which cannot be appealed.

Holiday Schedule

Dan and Linda agree to share holidays, birthdays and other important events on an approximately equal basis. Both agree that there should be at least one month's planning around the holiday schedule and for summer vacation, and they agree to notify the other by May 1 of each year concerning their summer vacation plans for the children.

Other Parenting Agreements

1. If there develops a question about which school district the children should attend, they will return to mediation.
2. If either parent must travel for work, both agree that the other parent is to care for the children.
3. If either parent must move out of state, both agree to return to mediation.
4. Illness of a child requires that the parent scheduled to have the child care for her.

They understand that the weekly schedule with each parent, as well as the holiday schedule, may need to be revised due to illnesses or emergencies. They agree to be flexible in responding to the needs of the other parent about parenting and scheduling, but they also agree not to use flexibility as a way of defeating the intent and purpose of the schedules.

They also agree to the concept of allowing each to provide parenting during the times they are scheduled to care for the children. This means that if the children are ill or Linda or Dan have other obligations during the scheduled time with the children, it will be the responsibility of the parent who is scheduled to be with the children to stay home from work and care for the children if they are sick. Both welcome the other parent to request assistance during their scheduled times with the children, but both understand that if the other parent is not able to assist them during the scheduled time with each parent, it will be the responsibility of the parent requesting assistance to make alternative arrangements for the children. Both agree that the children may decide to be with the parent not scheduled should the scheduled parent be out of town or unavailable to the children for whatever reason.

Health Insurance

Dan has health insurance through (_____), his employer. He agrees to continue to name the children as dependents on the policy and he will be responsible for providing health insurance coverage for the benefit of the children until he no longer has an obligation to share in the cost of raising the children. Dan agrees to ensure that Linda is supplied with current health insurance identification cards for the children.

In addition, they agree to take advantage of recent changes in Minnesota Statutes which allow for Linda to continue to be covered as a dependent on Dan's family health insurance policy after the entry of Dissolution. Both understand that such continued coverage is available to Linda only until either remarries or until Dan is no longer covered under the terms of the policy. Dan agrees to provide Linda with at least 90 days notice of his intent to remarry so that she can convert such coverage to a policy of individual coverage if she so chooses.

Uncovered medical and dental costs will be shared in the following manner: Linda will pay the first $300.00 of uncovered medical and prescription expenses incurred on behalf of the children in any calendar year. Uncovered expenses in excess of $300.00 will be shared on a pro-rata basis according to their incomes. Dan will be responsible for payment of all uncovered dental and orthodontia expenses incurred on behalf of the children during their minority.

Expenses

During the mediation process, Linda and Dan have examined their expenses individually as well as for the children. Their basic monthly expenses are attached in the appendix to this Memorandum of Agreement.

Linda has a high school diploma and is employed as a part-time secretary. Her present monthly net income is approximately $300.00.

Dan has an M.B.A. degree and is employed by (_____) as a sales manager. His monthly net income is approximately $3,034.00.

Their joint tax returns for the 1985 tax year are attached.

Child Support and Spousal Support

For child support, Dan will pay to Linda the sum of $500.00 per child per month, payable in equal installments on the first and fifteenth of each month until each minor child reaches age 18 or graduates from high school, whichever occurs later. They further agree that their Decree of Dissolution will contain a standard cost of living adjustment (COLA) except that the adjustments will occur only if the index increases and there will be no decrease in child support payments if the cost of living index decreases.

Based upon a tax analysis completed by their accountant, the $1,000.00-per-month child support payments represent approximately 30% of Dan's current net monthly income. They agree that upon their oldest child reaching age 18 or graduating from high school, child support will be reduced to 25% of Dan's net income.

Both agree that if any substantial changes occur that affect their support arrangements, they will first return to mediation before seeking relief in court.

For spousal support, they have agreed that Dan will pay $800.00 per month for a period of four years from the date of entry of Decree of Dissolution. The spousal support payments will terminate upon Linda's death, her remarriage or the expiration of four years from the date of entry of Decree of Dissolution.

They have reviewed the report of their accountant and understand that the combined child support and spousal support payments amount to approximately 50% of Dan's net income. Both agree that such arrangement is fair based upon the length of the marriage and based upon the fact that Linda deferred her education in order to assist Dan in completing his graduate M.B.A. degree.

(The Memorandum of Agreement continues to spell out the terms of their property division and is omitted from this case analysis. The substance of their property division called for an equal division of all assets with the exception of Linda receiving a larger portion of their savings to be used to pay tuition payments for three years of nurse's training. The entire property division agreement resulted in a 56% distribution of property to Linda and a 44% distribution to Dan).

CONCLUSION

The review and implementation process by their attorneys proceeded without complications except that Linda's attorney raised the issue of reserving spousal support beyond the four-year cut-off date. Dan's attorney resisted, pointing out the unequal property division award. The issue was settled when Linda informed her attorney that she did not wish to complicate the implementation of the final agreement. She has joined Parents Without Partners and has started dating. Dan continues to see the children on a slightly expanded schedule, being somewhat limited by the demands of Linda's school. The total cost for mediation came to $1,300.00. The cost for the attorneys review and implementation was $675.00 and the accountant's review cost $425.00.

4

Ron and Sue:
A Spousal Abuse
Relationship in
Divorce Mediation

INTRODUCTION

We felt it important to include a case study of a divorce where spousal abuse was present in the marriage relationship. Mediation of these types of cases has been controversial. Critics claim that spousal abuse divorces cannot be mediated due to the perceived unequal power of the spouses. In our practice, however, we have never excluded divorce clients with a history of domestic abuse. In fact, in approximately 700 divorces mediated during the 10 years of our practice, we believe that some physical abuse occurred in most of those marriage relationships. Though we did not routinely ask about physical abuse in the marriage relationship, many revealed that hitting, pushing and slapping occurred. Interestingly, they did not consider that to be physical abuse. (The extent of physical abuse is only now being investigated as we survey all of our past clients with the specific questions about the marriage relationship.)

Those couples who actually disclosed that physical abuse had occurred were not prevented from engaging in mediation provided both agreed to all standard Rules of Mediation. In the past, 12 couples acknowledged wife battering of a severity that ranged from hitting and throwing things to beatings that occurred the entire length of the marriage. By employing special procedures for these cases, eight have settled and four are still in progress. Demographic and settlement data on those eight cases are presented in Table 1.

Our supplementary procedures for mediating spousal abuse cases are as follows:

1. **Obtaining information:** An intake questionnaire is filled out by each spouse prior to the initial consultation. There is one question about abuse in the marriage relationship. This information is not shared with the other spouse, though it is raised by the mediator in the consultation.
2. **Safety of the victim:** We ask about safety of the battered wife and the children. If there is not an Order for Protection we ask, "What do the two of you need to do to assure that the abuse will not recur in the future?" Husbands usually reply that they will not "touch her ever again, after all, they're getting a di-

Table 1
Cases in Which Spousal Abuse Was Disclosed

Case letter	A	B	C	D	E	F	G	H
Case #	84166	85444	85455	86200	86655	86999	87066	87399
Age H	37	37	41	32	40	35	44	40
Age W	34	34	38	30	35	42	42	45
Years Married	16	14	15	10	14	11	22	17
Income H	24,600.00	36,000.00	37,000.00	38,000.00	46,000.00	35,000.00	32,000.00	34,000.00
Income W	10,000.00	6,000.00	-0-	41,200.00	4,800.00	20,000.00	20,000.00	15,000.00
County H	Hennepin	Anoka	Dakota	Hennepin	Hennepin	WI	Hennepin	Hennepin
County W	Anoka	Cedar	Apple Valley	Plymouth	Mpls	N/A	New Hope	Plymouth
City H	Brk Ctr	Anoka	Dakota	Hennepin	Hennepin	WI	Hennepin	Hennepin
City W	Anoka	Coon Rapids	Apple Valley	Mpls	Mpls	N/A	New Hope	Plymouth
Chn #	three	four	two	none	three	two	three	two
Ages	13, 10, 7	11, 10, 8, 7	11, 6	N/A	12, 9, 5	8, 6	20, 17, 15	10, 6
Counseling H	Yes	Yes	Yes	Yes	No	Yes	Yes	No
Counseling W	Yes	Yes	Yes	Yes	No	Yes	Yes	No
Joint Counseling	Yes	Yes	Yes	No	Yes	Yes	Yes	Yes
Legal Process H	No	Yes	No	No	No	Yes	Yes	No
Legal Process W	No	Yes	No	No	No	Yes	Yes	No
Lawyer Retained H	No	Yes	No	Yes	Yes	Yes	Yes	No
Lawyer Retained W	No	Yes	No	Yes	Yes	Yes	Yes	No
Alimony $	N/A	No	266.00/mo	No	300.00/mo	N/A	N/A	100.00/mo
Paid to	W	n/a	W	N/A	W	N/A	N/A	W
Child Support $	350.00/mo	800.00/mo	634.00/mo	N/A	700.00/mo	N/A	N/A	450.00/mo
Paid to	W	W	W	N/A	W	N/A	N/A	W
Legal Custody	Joint	Joint	Joint	N/A	Joint	Joint	Joint	Joint
Physical Custody	W	W	W	N/A	Joint	W	N/A	W
Parenting Arrangements	80W/20H	70W/30H	80W/20H	N/A	50W/50H	50W/50H	N/A	79W/21H
Domestic Abuse Services	Yes	Yes	No	No	Yes	Yes	No	No
Order for Protection	Yes	Yes	No	Yes	Yes	Yes	Yes	No

vorce." Regardless of the husband's promises, wives remain fearful of any encounter with the husband, especially at their home. Therefore, we always discuss seriously the need for an Order for Protection, explaining its purpose and how it is obtained. Husbands routinely object to the need for such an Order. However, the husband's understanding and cooperation can be obtained by reminding him that the Order will have no adverse consequences if he follows through on his promise not to abuse her.

3. **Safety of the children:** We also ask whether the children have been abused or are at risk for abuse. Most often, both will answer that the children have been emotionally affected from witnessing the violence and verbal abuse. If there has been physical abuse of the children, we ask both to be specific about what they mean. It is extremely important to determine if the abuse is still occurring. If so, we inform them that the abuse must be reported to the Child Protection authorities. We then work on a procedure for reporting—who will report, will they voluntarily report and ask for help, etc.

   If they express the desire to resolve this immediately, referral to a child psychologist on an emergency basis while the report is being made to child protection is a wise choice. (This again avoids the need to dwell on fault with one parent in order to begin to resolve the problem. They can cooperate for the sake of the children.) In order to preserve our professional relationship, we can make the report to child protection with their full knowledge and understanding.

4. **Resolving spousal abuse:** Another special rule we require is that the couple be involved in therapy or a special program dealing with the spousal abuse issues.

They both must commit to such a course or the mediation will be terminated. If they are not already in therapy or treatment, we will refer them and follow up to
confirm their attendance.

5. **Contact between spouses:** Contact between the husband and wife outside the mediation office is an important concern. Usually, the first topic for discussion
is an attempt to convince the husband that his wife is
serious in her pursuit of the divorce, and therefore does
not wish to see him. Husbands often have difficulty
accepting this notion because in abusive relationships
they are accustomed to controlling the wife's every
move. Potential problems are the contact which occurs
around the exchanges of the children and when the
wife is confronted with home maintenance problems.
In mediation we discuss and decide exactly what type
of contact they will have outside the sessions as well
as the frequency of contact. They are also asked to establish rules for the immediate termination of contact
should violence erupt, or even if one simply becomes
uncomfortable in the other's presence. We ask them
to be very specific, and they are provided with a written memorandum of agreement to avoid as much confusion and misunderstanding as possible.

6. **Boundaries and privacy:** Related to the above discussion of contact, boundaries go beyond the contact to
specific agreement about their separateness. We promote the reality that divorce means that they will no
longer be husband and wife. Until the divorce is final,
they must live separately and begin to be independent
of each other. This is particularly difficult for the couple who have been in an abusive relationship. The co-
dependent nature of that enmeshed relationship is hard
to change. In mediation, we are asking them to agree

upon the terms of their independence from each other.

Frequently, the house becomes the focal point for such boundary discussions. If the wife is living in the home, the husband may feel that he has the right to enter at will because it is his property or, "there are some of my things still in the house." At this point it is important to stress their separateness as well as respect for each other's privacy. We encourage them to honor each other's privacy and we encourage a rule which prevents access to the other's home without prior agreement.

These preliminary rules are a necessary foundation to successful mediation of divorces where spousal abuse is present. Confronting the spousal abuse issues early allows for "smoother sailing" throughout the remainder of the mediation process, as well as for protection of the parties. Even though these issues have been addressed at the beginning of mediation, they may need to be reclarified upon the request of either party later in the process. With the facts of the abuse out in the open, an agreement for action as well as protection is in place. While no judgments have been made, the agreements and commitments made tend to keep problems in check while mediation is completed.

Several trends appear in this type of case. We have found that when such couples elect to enter mediation, they need to learn different methods of negotiating in order to place them on equal footing with each other. As mediators we find ourselves working much harder to influence changes in their attitudes towards cooperation. It must be remembered that they probably have had little experience with engaging in cooperative behavior, let alone cooperative negotiations, during the marriage. In most of these cases, the wife is the initiator of the divorce. Wives have the opportunity to be more optimistic when they see a positive process for termination of the marriage that does not punish their husbands but also does not relieve their responsibility as husbands for the battering of the past. Safety is a primary concern and threats by either party are investigated as to the underlying, unstated need or concern. Once threats are unraveled to discover their real message, they are more easily resolved in mediation.

Mediating spousal abuse cases is more difficult for the mediator, and generally takes more time than the usual six- to 10-hour average per case. The terms of their settlement outcomes do not appear to be significantly different from other cases. However, the parties usually will have gained a much clearer understanding of the dynamics of their past relationship. Hopefully, they have learned a more positive way to relate to each other in the future parenting exchanges and contacts. We have found husbands to be remorseful, even wishing that they could start all over again with the marriage. However, we know of no couples so far that have remarried each other after the divorce.

RON AND SUE: FACTUAL BACKGROUND

Ron and Sue, ages 36 and 34 respectively, were married in 1969 about 20 miles from where they presently reside. They have three children: Kathy, age 13; Heather, age 10; and Jessie, age 7. Ron has been employed full time in office management with the same employer since 1966. He earns a gross annual income of $24,600.00. Ron is a high school graduate and has three post high school certificates in Welding, Auto Mechanics and Small Engines. Sue has been employed part time as a school bus driver since 1976. Her hourly rate of pay is $12.35 and her gross annual income was $7,684.00 for the year before entering mediation. She has had no further specialized training since her high school diploma. However, she has two years experience as a drafter and has an interest in graphic design.

They describe their years of marriage as consisting of good memories and very bad ones. The bad memories are of when Ron was drinking heavily. He often had blackouts and would beat Sue, not remembering anything the next morning. He would become very remorseful and guilty about hurting her. He also caused great damage to the home during these blackouts and the children frequently witnessed his violent rampages. Sue had been treated several times for her injuries and she finally obtained an Order for Protection which required him to vacate the home. As a part of her action, Ron went into treatment for his alcoholism, and has remained sober since.

They reconciled, but found that the intense anger and intimidation were still present. Sue was continually fearful of his outbursts, even though the physical abuse did not recur. Ron attends AA meetings five nights a week just to keep sober. He understands his emotional recovery is going to take a long time, but he is committed to it. Sue subsequently brought an action for divorce and they came to mediation because they did not want to fight any more.

Ron never physically abused the children. However, the children were certainly traumatized by the violence and also by his anger aimed at them through verbal and emotional abuse. Their daughter, Kathy, often took on the role of caretaker for her mother, and she has withdrawn from her father. She was having academic and behavior problems in school, and would seek out her close group of friends for support when she became upset with life at home. She stayed away from home and kept to herself when at home. This type of distancing which places emotional and physical space between an adolescent and his/her parents is not uncommon in a divorce situation (Wallerstein & Kelly, 1980).

Heather was caught in the middle of the conflict between her parents, and tried very hard to please her dad and be close to her mom. Jessie was the charmer of the family with her cute behavior. She attracted attention to herself in stressful moments to ease the tension, and in an attempt to find security for herself in a family that was coming apart.

Ron and Sue own their home in a lower middle class suburb about 25 miles northeast of Minneapolis. It is valued at $65,000.00 by a real estate appraisal, and has a mortgage against it with a balance of $18,000.00 owing. Considering all of the encumbrances against it and the selling costs, Ron and Sue agree that it has a net equity of $34,000.00. This is their major asset. Others include: cash value on insurance policies of $2,287.00; an IRA balance of $1,812.00; three motor vehicles worth $7,875.00; a boat, canoe and tent trailer worth a total of $3,300.00, and personal property, furnishings, tools and miscellaneous objects with a total value of $7,470.00. They also have two loans with combined balances owing of $3,520.00. Their marital net worth is approximately $54,000.00.

INTAKE PROCEDURE

Ron initiated the contact with the mediation office by phone. In his initial conversation he stated that he did not want the divorce, but if it was going to happen, he hoped he and his wife could remain friends afterwards. He called back to make an appointment after receiving the informational packet.

At the initial consultation, Sue was very quiet and Ron appeared sad and nervous. Sue sat slouched in her chair and looked down much of the time. Ron sat up in a very rigid posture and responded to questions with short answers. His voice was intense when he spoke, while Sue spoke so softly that at times it was difficult to hear her. Through the comments of both about the marriage relationship, it became clear that chemical abuse and spousal abuse were part of their history.

The relationship between chemical abuse and spousal abuse is well known. Deschner (1983) reported that 72% of those surveyed in her study were abusing alcohol or drugs (p. 9) and that ". . . drinking and family violence appear to have an association that is far greater than chance" (p. 31).

During the initial meeting, the following exchange occurred which highlights the problem for mediators when facing spousal abuse cases:

> Sue seemed guilt-ridden for insisting on the divorce, yet firm in her words spoken quietly towards the floor, "I've forgiven you, but I can't forget." Ron responded, "Do you still care about me?", to which she nodded assent. He then said, "I still believe we can make this thing work if we both really try."

The constant attempts by Ron to seek Sue's forgiveness present a difficult dilemma for Sue. If she agrees with his statement that the marriage will work if "we really try," she then is portrayed as bad for pursuing the divorce now that he is really trying to change. However, Ron fails to recognize that the divorce is a direct result of his abuse and victimization of her. As the mediation continues, Ron can alleviate his own guilt by pointing out that "she does not even want to try to work on the marriage relationship." In a reversal of what would be expected, he proceeds to play a victim's role and attempts to justify a settlement in his favor and against her. In most divorces, the spouse not initiating the divorce seems to use fault (that is, the other is at fault for breaking the Marriage Contract) to argue for a more generous settlement favoring the non-initiator.

To understand the implications of this entire verbal exchange and make sense of it as the process continues, Sue must be given support and not faulted for making her choice to end the marriage. This support can be given through a series of questions to Ron:

Mediator: Ron, do you understand why she does not want to try again? Can you respect her need to proceed with the divorce? Is it possible that her request is not a reflection on you and she is not blaming you, but doing what she sees as most healthy for herself right now?

Ron: I understand but I don't have to like it, do I?

Mediator: No, and I appreciate your willingness to accept this. Is the protection order still in effect?

Sue: Yes.

Ron: I haven't come near you since I've been sober, have I?

Sue: No, you haven't and I'm grateful for that, but I am still afraid of you, and I don't know what you will do when you come to pick up the kids.

After this exchange we talked about how the emotional outbursts create fear and tension which cause Sue to feel threatened and to hear the old tapes replaying inside her head. Ron put his head in his hands trying hard to wipe the tears before they were visible and said he understood. Sue cried, too, and said she wished it didn't have to be this way. At this point we continued to discuss the mediation process. We deviated frequently from my usual script for a consultation, because of the concerns raised with each issue:

Ron: What should I do about my income? Do I keep it and continue to pay the bills?

Sue: How do I know what bills he is paying, he never talks to me.

Ron: I don't know why you want the Jeep, it doesn't work and you can't fix it.

Sue: My friend, Larry, said he can fix it for nothing.

Ron: I don't want him touching anything!

Mediator: That will probably be one of the first issues we will work on. Getting divorced means you will need to separate the bills and property. It is good to begin to get some of these issues settled first, at least temporarily, so you each know what is being paid for and by whom so we can then get on with the rest of the issues to be decided in the divorce.

Consultations generally last one hour in length, but Ron and Sue used close to two hours. At the end of the consultation, they agreed to proceed with mediation. As both had already talked with attorneys, Sue shared that she was intimidated by her attorney because he was suggesting that she "go after" Ron and get everything they had.

Ron's attorney advised him to seek possession of the house and children by showing that Sue was unstable and had neglected the children. Prior to entering mediation, Ron had called child protection and reported that Sue had left the children alone overnight. His attorney advised this was excellent ammunition for his winning custody of the children, yet Ron said he did not want to do that to Sue. Sue also said she did not like her attorney's attitude and, as with many couples who enter mediation, they put their attorneys on the back burner.

Both agreed that mediation could better achieve their goal of maintaining respect for each other as well as remaining good parents to the children after the divorce. "The children have suffered enough already," Sue said. Coming back to the safety issue, it was important to ask Sue if she felt she could make good decisions in mediation and not be intimidated by Ron. She responded that she felt better talking to Ron in mediation than she had felt in a long time, and that this would work best for both of them. Ron said he could see that I was not taking Sue's side as he had feared, and that I was being fair with both of them. I agreed with them that I felt this would work well for both and especially for their children.

I asked them to each continue with counseling and I explained that through counseling it was possible to learn about the dynamics of their own relationship. This in turn would help them in future relationships. Sue indicated that she had dropped out of counseling, but was willing to begin Alanon again. Ron agreed to continue attendance at an AA program and they both agreed to take the children to Alateen or family counseling. I told them I felt mediation would work only if they continued these programs, and since they were willing, I would agree to mediate their divorce.

Each was given a set of rules and we discussed the formal and informal rules of mediation. I pointed out that the rules made mediation a safe and fair environment and I emphasized rules of confidentiality and full disclosure, as crucial for success. I stressed that they must be open and honest about sharing information and their actions around use of assets and acquiring debt in order to build trust and make lasting decisions:

1. They would not be allowed to attack each other verbally or emotionally in this room, and I would stop this from happening if I recognized it. I talked about how they each knew the buttons they could push to hurt the other, which I might not recognize, and they each must tell me when that was occurring so I could end it. Sue and Ron both admitted that they knew how and what buttons to push to cause the other pain, and both agreed they would try not to do so.
2. They would speak in the first person with "I" statements, and not speak for each other.
3. I do not allow any angry outbursts, and if they occurred I would recess the session for five or 10 minutes.
4. I asked them not to call me between sessions, that if they had something they felt I should know, they would talk to my assistant who would take care of it or consult with me. I also gave them each a questionnaire to fill out in preparation for the first sessions and set an appointment for two weeks later.

5. I asked them not to talk with each other between sessions except about items that were discussed in mediation.

As a footnote to all of this, after the first working session I noticed that Sue answered, "Do you have an interest in reconciliation?" on the mediation questionnaire with a question mark, and left most of the other questions blank. Ron also left that question unanswered. The next three working sessions were filled with countless examples of their ambivalence and indecision about the marriage relationship. Spousal abuse couples seem so much like the Ancient Mariner, floundering amidst violent storms with a great albatross around their necks. Yet, when asked if they want it removed, they say, "I don't know." Therefore, the role of the mediator in the actual working sessions is to clearly outline their choices and the consequences of each choice while at the same time permitting them to make the choices. The next section of this case study explains our conceptual approach in working with couples who have a history of spousal abuse.

CONCEPTUAL FRAMEWORK USED TO ANALYZE AND MEDIATE THIS CASE

General Approach and Special Considerations

I approached this case much the same as mediating any other case except for a special need to constantly monitor the power, guilt, and subtle hidden agendas of each party. Their past communication style was very dysfunctional. A pattern of dishonesty, threats and coercion eventually resulted in violence and victimization—Ron through physical and emotional abuse, intimidation and manipulation and Sue through retaliation by using friends, neighbors, police or the order for protection in any way she could exert power over him.

Even in their therapy groups, both obtained support for their own predicament, thus reinforcing their win-lose competitive stance towards each other. In order to promote a more cooperative approach, I attempted to eliminate or reduce blaming communication. I encouraged them to be future-focused by trying to concentrate on their needs and interests and not on fault. Finding fault is a negative activity that keeps the couple enmeshed in the negative intimacies of the past. I urged Ron and Sue to learn a more constructive way of communicating with each other, and I had to intervene frequently during the early meetings to stop inappropriate communication. Most often this involved restating their concerns and issues in less blaming, future-focused statements.

Since I also consider spousal abuse a life-threatening situation, it was necessary to take extreme steps by asking for commitments from them to assure their safety outside of the mediation sessions. These steps consisted of written agreements about boundaries and privacy, as well as procedures for action if these were violated.

One question I always address is whether they will communicate with each other outside of the mediation room. In this case, Ron and Sue needed to communicate about the children and the exchanges between homes. One of the games they had played very well was the "hit and miss" game. They would agree on the time that Ron was to pick up the children and if he was not there on time, Sue would put her car in the garage, turn out the lights, lock the doors, and pretend that no one was home.

On the other hand, Ron would often call and say that he would be an hour late and interfere with her plans. If she left the children with a babysitter to wait when he was late, he would verbally attack her about her lack of judgment in choosing a person to be with the children. When I asked them how they thought the children felt when these things happened, both immediately agreed that the children were the ultimate losers.

Although these issues surface in many divorce mediation cases, with the history of abuse and violence in this case, it was necessary to help them take small positive steps. First we worked on how they could make the changes of the children work better and how the children should be helped in adjusting to their parent's separation. I began by focusing on a regular recurring schedule of times when the children would be with Ron. They agreed that until everything else was settled, the children would spend every other weekend with Ron and two evenings each week. I then asked about the specific times of exchange and location—was it permissible for Ron to pick the children up at the house? Ron complained about the presence of Sue's boyfriend and after some discussion Sue agreed that she would replace the boyfriend by another adult friend who she felt was needed for safety reasons. Ron objected, and again I repeated my efforts through the following interventions (description of each mediator intervention is italicized in parentheses):

Mediator: Sue, can you explain to Ron why you want to have another adult present when he comes over to pick up the children? *(Clarification of Sue's needs statement.)*

Sue: I am afraid that Ron will want to come into the house and talk to me, and I don't want him to because he always wants to try to get me to change my mind and get back together with him.

Mediator: Ron, do you understand what Sue is saying? *(Checking out with Ron if he understood Sue's needs statement.)*

Ron: Yes, but we never have any time to talk, and if only we could talk I think things could work out. I'm not the same as I used to be. I don't want to lose my family. (He begins to cry, head in hands and bent forward in his chair.)

Sue: But you know I don't want to talk about that. We are getting a divorce.

Mediator: Ron, do you understand why Sue doesn't want you to come into the house. *(Narrowing the needs statement to a boundary issue.)*

Sue: Ron, I don't want to give you any false hopes, we both hurt enough already.

Ron: I guess you're right, I've just got to learn to accept this—it's too hard—it hurts so much. In AA they tell you to make amends to those you have hurt. I've made amends to Sue, but it doesn't change anything. I know I shouldn't expect her to forgive me after what I've done but I wish things could work out for us.

Mediator: Ron, can you accept picking the children up and not stepping into the house? *(Focusing on the original concern.)*

Ron: Yes, I guess I'll have to. But I don't want to just sit in the driveway, can't I at least come up to the door?

Sue: Yes, I guess that would be OK if you promise not to come in.

Mediator: You have each given here—Ron, you've agreed not to come into the house, and Sue, you've agreed that Ron can come up to the door when picking up the children. These are ways that the two of you can begin to build trust as well as a parenting relationship that will be helpful to the children. Perhaps there will be a day when you can say a few words to each other at the door about the children without the tension that you now feel as you anticipate these exchanges. *(Validation and summary of agreements.)* After all, you two are divorcing each other but you will have a parenting relationship for a long time. *(Promoting reality.)* Let's talk about the time of the exchanges and see if we can clear up any problems around exchange times. *(Focusing and narrowing of issues.)*

This type of interchange occurred frequently. As each such issue surfaced, I helped them redefine the dispute in its narrowest terms. This forced them to deal with the narrow issue of the exchange—not the emotional issues of loss of marriage or past hurts.

Each small agreement became part of their larger settlement. More importantly, making and carrying out these agreements (rather than being ordered to do something by a judge) allowed them to proceed into the future with new skills to relate to each other as parents. Building their agreements step by step with issues other than parenting ultimately had the effect of assisting them to unhook from being marriage partners because they confronted the reality of the divorce each time they added a new agreement that got them closer to totally separate living.

The concept of mutuality is especially complex in cases of spousal abuse. I try to promote their being "in the soup together" and encourage them to work together to emerge with the most constructive settlement possible. However, I must be careful not to reinforce the abuser's hidden agenda. In this case it was Ron's desire "to stay in the soup together." Sue is trying to escape from a relationship that has become deeply enmeshed in negative intimacies and psychological dependency/control issues. Without a great deal of effort, Sue will stay enmeshed.

To change this relationship, I work intensively with them to change their attitudes by promoting the reality that they are working on their divorce, not the improvement of the marriage relationship (as illustrated in the above narrative, "After all, the two of you are divorcing each other . . ."). I monitor their communication in the room to keep it assertive, not aggressive. When aggressive or coercive statements are made, I restate them in more neutral terminology asking if that is what was meant. Ron's coercive statements to Sue no longer contained the overt threat of physical abuse, but Ron tried to convince her that her actions were emotionally abusive to him. This had the potential of making Sue feel she was victimizing him by seeking the divorce. By failing to stop the coercive communication, Sue may have eventually abandoned the divorce, and returned to the former marriage relationship as so many battered women do when trying to separate or divorce the batterer (Roy, 1977).

Differences Between Mediation and Counseling

As a general rule, mediators are more successful when they focus on the future and avoid the past. Therapy deliberately delves into the past because its goal is to resolve something in the past that is causing problems. The goal of divorce mediation is to obtain an agreement between two people, not to resolve the past. Mediation is a decision-making process for couples in divorce who cannot decide all of the divorce issues between themselves and choose not to enlist the adversarial process as their method of decision-making. The assistance of a third-party neutral mediator allows them to maintain control over the outcome of their issues, thereby obtaining ownership of the decisions. The role of the mediator is to guide them through a structured problem-solving process that ends in settlement. The need for therapy surfaces in mediation when the emotions of the parties interfere with the decision-making process.

In spousal abuse cases as well as in some non-abuse cases, a referral to therapy is necessary to enhance the couple's ability to mediate. I always assume that along with violence there are hurt, anger, and lack of understanding and communication. One spouse, in this case Ron, does not want the divorce, and because of that maintains his denial even while mediating the divorce. While I teach new skills and patterns of communication, Ron and Sue need to understand why Sue insists on the divorce—why she has resolved that divorce is the only way for her to grow and change. That is not an issue for mediation, it is one that will be dealt with in therapy for both of them.

Therapy is a process where each party comes to terms with the reasons for the divorce. They have an opportunity in therapy to wrestle with their personal and relationship problems and look into their pasts, not to find fault, but to learn why they have come to this point. They then can each begin to learn ways that they can be different and what they have to do to alleviate the hurt and anger and to not use those emotions so destructively any more.

It is true that mediation calls upon some of the same techniques that are used in therapy. However, the techniques are employed in mediation to resolve settlement roadblocks, whereas therapy has a different goal. While the therapists work with the internal psychological problems, mediators work with the more immediate, concrete issues of children, money and property.

Mediators do not need to take long histories of the past problems that led to the decision to divorce. That would take a long time and would lend little to the resolution of the divorce issues. Rather, mediators need to acquire knowledge about housing, money and property in order to assist the couple in their decision-making. However, a good mediator must have a solid understanding of the emotional divorce the couple is experiencing. It is important to understand that the emotional divorce begins earlier with one party than with the other, so that when one spouse is asking for the divorce, the other has probably not yet seriously considered divorce.

I remind couples that no matter who took the first step towards divorce, they both have been involved in the breakdown of the marriage relationship, because marriages do not fall apart overnight. Ron was alcoholic when he and Sue married, though neither was aware of it. They grew enmeshed in a dysfunctional relationship that grew more violent with the years. Now, on the threshold of divorce, they are each aware of how they arrived at this threshold. Ron prefers to continue being married to Sue, and Sue prefers to discontinue the relationship. Ron needs to understand and accept Sue's reasons so as not to manipulate her in mediation by faulting her in the decision-making process.

This is an extremely important point for mediators. The difference between therapy and mediation is that Ron's acceptance of and respect for Sue's choice to terminate the marriage result in better negotiations between the two of them in mediation. The therapist may have a goal of helping both change their behavior to prevent future dysfunctional relationships with other partners, but the mediator's goal of growth and change is to facilitate the ability to negotiate. As such, different techniques are used by the mediator, although a helpful adjunct to mediation may very well be the referral to therapy.

Ron and Sue were in Alcoholics Anonymous and Alanon, respectively, during the mediation process to work on their relationship and personal issues. In addition, Ron agreed in mediation to go into family counseling with the children to improve his relationship with them. Sue also attended a support group for battered women. Ron additionally worked "one day at a time" on his addiction to alcohol, which he described as a tremendous "fight to stay sober." Sue attended Alanon once a week; Ron went to AA meetings five nights a week. When extreme anger and emotions surfaced in the mediation room, I asked them to raise the issue in their respective groups for help and support. I also asked for permission to talk with their counselors if necessary, and I explained that I would need consent forms signed by each of them. They each agreed. However, it was never necessary to contact their counselors.

CRITICAL ISSUES PRESENTED

Five major issues relating to the violent nature of their marriage relationship were critical to the settlement of the case. These issues were: (1) husband's control; (2) setting boundaries; (3) letting go; (4) lack of funds; and (5) parenting.

1. Husband's Control

Ron's need to have control over each issue was very evident and caused many feelings of mistrust and suspicion. When valuing items of property, Ron would first try to get Sue to agree who would get it, before discussing values. If it was to be awarded to him, he minimized the value and if it was to be awarded to her, he talked about how much it meant to him, and then gave it an inflated value. Ron became very frustrated with my rule of value first, then divide. For example, they owned a tent camper, and neither knew its value. When I asked about its value, Ron said, "It doesn't matter, she can have it." I then stated the rule and asked how they could get a value. She said she could take it to a dealer who sells used campers and get a value. Ron challenged her on how she could get it to a dealer without a trailer hitch. She said she could borrow a friend's car with a hitch. He then said she had no idea what it was worth and that the dealer would talk her into selling it to him "for a song" and she would agree. I intervened and clarified that getting a value did not mean she would sell it. Sue agreed that she had no intention of selling it, and if Ron wanted it in the divorce settlement it was fine with her. Ron then responded with, "Be sure to show him [the dealer] the rip in the roof." Then he said he didn't believe she'd get a fair appraisal because she did not know what it was worth. I asked him what he thought it was worth and he refused, tossing the question to Sue, who very timidly said, "between $1,200.00 and $1,500.00." Ron said, "Fine, take it to the dealer, but I won't agree to anything less than $1,200.00."

This is only one example of Ron's attempt to control the process and outcome during mediation. As he trusted the process more and felt his needs being met through consistent rules being applied, his negotiating behavior improved.

2. Setting Boundaries

This is one issue that emerged at every session, and a review of the videotape allowed me to see how it was progressively resolved from session to session. The first time it surfaced, Ron asked Sue for a key to the house so he could get some of his things out. Sue became upset, stared at the floor and barely got out the words, "No, I don't want you to have a key to the house." I spoke first, restating what Sue had said and then simply asked, "Why?" Apparently, both felt guilty about this issue. (I later learned that it reminded Ron of his violent behavior, while Sue felt she was depriving Ron of entry to his home.) Each subsequent time the key was discussed, Sue spoke more loudly and clearly. About the third time, she actually looked at Ron when she said it. At the same time, Ron became less demanding in his tone of voice. The last time, Sue sat up straight and looked Ron in the eyes and said, "No, you can't have the keys until I move out because I still don't trust you." Ron finally gave up and said nothing.

My role in this exchange was to be patient. Each time it arose, there seemed to be more respect for the idea of Sue's boundary needs. I was careful not to take sides, but

rather pushed them to continue talking until it was resolved. Ron truly felt that he was trustworthy. Although
Sue wished she could trust him, both needed the opportunity to exchange views. In this critical issue, I was able
to help Ron understand the things he must do differently
to gain back Sue's trust. By asking Sue to begin looking
for ways she could trust him, I was able to also be very
supportive of her unwillingness to provide him a key. By
supporting both issues (his trustworthiness and her
boundaries), each gained more confidence in the process.

3. Letting Go

Ron stated from the beginning of mediation that he did
not want this divorce. Sue definitely wanted it, but was
occasionally ambivalent. She talked about the weight of
that decision, and frequently questioned her decision. She
was fearful about what it would do to the children, and
about finances. As long as she and Ron made good decisions about the children, she felt strong about her decision. If Ron questioned her parenting or complained that
the children were suffering from the divorce, she weak-
ened. My role, then, was to focus on the children to find
solutions that met both of their needs as parents. I asked
them to experiment with several exchange schedules and
I suggested the children be in counseling. When they finally negotiated a fair parenting plan, Sue strongly stressed
the need to proceed with the divorce.

4. Lack of Funds

Whether families are affluent or impoverished, one of
the biggest adjustments for them when they divorce sur-

rounds finances. In this case, there simply wasn't enough money for Ron and Sue to live the lifestyle they had enjoyed while married. They owned a three-bedroom home which Ron insisted was too expensive for Sue to afford after the divorce. Sue, to Ron's surprise, did not wish to live in the house because of all the bad memories and unrepaired damage. The problem was not being poor, but rather poor monthly cash flow. Both were good about curtailing any unnecessary spending, and Sue worked more hours to earn more money, but they were both fearful of future finances. Sue looked for an apartment, but Ron objected to each one she found. Instead, she found a house to buy if Ron paid her half of the equity in their house. Ron did so, and Sue had a home for herself and the children, with a mortgage payment that was less than apartment rent.

It was still very difficult for each of them to make ends meet. For each problem that arose, I asked them to list several ways to solve it (option development) and then discuss each one and weigh the consequences. Their fears lessened as the finances became more manageable and decisions were carried out.

5. *Parenting*

During the marriage, Sue was the primary parent at home with the children. Only recently had Ron begun to assume a larger parenting role with the children. Sue felt that the children should have a good relationship with their father, but complained about him being rigid and nervous around them. Ron vacillated between feeling ineffectual with the children to suggesting that he have custody of the children and Sue visit them on weekends.

Ron's feelings seemed always to dictate his direction, instead of his taking a rational approach. They finally settled on a schedule for the children to be with Ron every other weekend and two evenings each week. Until Sue moved out of the house, he was unable to have the children overnight, but took them to his parents' home for the weekends. At first the children were not comfortable going with him, and he needed Sue's help in encouraging the children.

Ron often complained about Sue's easygoing style with the children and also accused her of neglecting them by leaving them home alone in the evenings. So, in addition to the schedules, Ron and Sue needed to adopt some rules about parenting. First they agreed that neither was neglecting or abusing the children. Sue found herself educating Ron about the children's habits, preferences and schedules. She also agreed to help the children understand and accept Ron and forgive both of them for the past violence. In each session they made small agreements about the children while continuing to follow the new schedule.

I asked the children to be present at the review session. In the presence of the entire family, I explained my work with their parents and then talked about how they were planning to take care of them from two homes. The children were quiet and clung to their parents. When we talked about the divorce, they cried and wished it did not have to be. As gently as I could, I said: "Mom and Dad cannot get along living together anymore. When they were together there was so much fighting that they decided it would be better that they got a divorce." The session was hard for Ron and Sue also because it seemed to put closure on the marriage for the entire family.

ROADBLOCKS AND DETOURS ON
THE ROAD TO SETTLEMENT

At this point the reader has a good picture of the case of Ron and Sue. The major roadblocks and how I dealt with them will now be easier to understand. (Major interventions are italicized within parentheses.)

1. Ron made Sue feel guilty for wanting the divorce by saying how hard it would be for the children, or that she did not give it a chance after he began his AA program. I repeatedly asked him to accept that Sue wanted the divorce, and questioned the fairness of this accusation. Ron always backed off, apologized, and said, "this is so hard" in a broken, emotional tone. *(Promoted reality and focused on fairness.)*
2. Ron suggested that since Sue could not afford to live in the house, he would keep the house and the children, and she could visit. This hurt Sue deeply. I questioned Ron as to how he would care for the children during work. He said Sue could come over to the house and take care of them. I asked them both how the children might respond to this arrangement and both said the children would be very confused. *(Promoted reality and mutuality.)*
3. Ron refused to pay spousal maintenance, saying, "Why should I pay her to live separately when I did not even agree with getting the divorce?" I asked them to consider their budgets and what each of them needed and then asked about what they felt was fair. Sue did not want spousal maintenance, only child support. She said her earnings were enough for her to live on. *(Focused on needs and interests and discussion of fairness.)*

4. Even after the mediation settlement, Ron made the divorce very difficult by questioning each step in the legal process. He stalled on delivering a quit claim deed to Sue and called me to explain why he should not sign. I asked him some questions to try to understand what he was conflicted about. Again he replied, "I know that if I sign this it will be all over." I responded with, "Ron, are you just delaying the inevitable?" He said, "Yes, I guess so, and it's really going to happen, isn't it?" He was still very sad. (*Identify true nature of the conflict, help parties accept their decisions.*)

SUMMARY OF SETTLEMENT REACHED

The following represents a summary of Sue and Ron's Memorandum of Agreement of the divorce settlement reached in mediation.

Parenting Issues

They agreed to have Joint Legal Custody of the children, which means that they will each continue to have the legal rights and obligations regarding the children after the divorce that they had while married. They will consult with each other and jointly decide all major decisions, which are usually about medical treatment, religious upbringing, and education of the children. In addition, the children will live primarily with Sue, and they will be with Ron every other weekend from Friday evening through Sunday evening, and one or two evenings each week until approximately 8:00 p.m.

They agreed to be open and flexible about changes in the parenting schedule. Ron may have the children with him more often or for longer periods of time based on the outcome of his counseling with the children. The schedule is meant to be a minimal amount of time for the children to be with Ron and is based upon his work and evening schedules. Each may have the children for blocks of time for vacations and trips, and those will be decided at least a month in advance.

They also agreed to share the holidays each year on an equal basis and alternate the holidays between them each year. The exception is that Ron will have the children with him every year on Christmas Eve, and Sue will have the children with her each year on Christmas Day, according to the traditions in their respective extended families.

Support Arrangements

Prior to beginning the first mediation session, Ron and Sue each prepared budgets of their living expenses amortized monthly as a basis. They figured the children's expenses according to who would be responsible for purchasing or paying for the specific needs. They considered the amount of time the children spent in each of their homes as affecting some budget categories (i.e. food, recreation, etc.). They finally agreed that Ron would pay Sue $800.00 per month as the base child support amount. They also agreed that this figure would be changed every two years based upon the change in the Consumer Price Index for the previous two years.

In addition, Ron would provide health insurance for the children and pay medical and dental expenses not covered by insurance.

Neither wanted spousal maintenance. Sue wanted to feel financially independent of Ron and did not want him to pay spousal support. She also felt that she would increase her income substantially from $6,000.00 per year to at least $10,000.00 gross annual income within the next year. This amount, plus the child support (which was not taxable to her) would provide enough income for her and the children to live a lifestyle similar to that during the marriage. She did ask for continued health insurance coverage under Ron's policy until the remarriage or death of either of them, which was the Minnesota law at the time. Ron agreed to be responsible for repayment of all the marital debts as part of the property settlement. This was very helpful to Sue.

With these support arrangements, Ron and Sue both came close to meeting their monthly budgetary expenses, and each was satisfied with the decisions.

Property Settlement

They agreed that they would divide all marital property equally. Since Sue had no interest in staying in the house, she agreed that it could be awarded to Ron if he would buy out her interest so she could purchase another house for herself and the children. Ron's father loaned Ron the money to pay Sue for her interest. As for the rest of their property, they valued each item before they decided who would own it after the divorce. Of their $54,000.000 net worth, each received approximately $27,000.00 in value.

CONCLUSION

Ron and Sue relied almost entirely upon the mediation process for settlement of their divorce. They each had retained attorneys, but neither consulted with their attorneys during the mediation process. Ron had a great disdain for attorneys in general, perhaps because he perceived them as controlling and threatening, characteristics similar to those he possessed. Sue felt the same, but rather than have her attorney take on the role of her "protector" in the divorce, she chose to be directly involved herself. Her reasoning for this was that it was best for the children, "They had been hurt enough already."

Much of the criticism leveled at the mediation process for mediating cases of spousal abuse surrounds the issue of protection for the victim. The case of Ron and Sue demonstrates that it is possible to empower the victim to become stronger and more confident in negotiating, and hopefully never need the "protection" again. The theory of "legal protection" of the victim does not allow for growth and empowerment, but instead may temporarily protect her through the divorce and then leave her unchanged to enter into another such relationship later. It actually encourages a dependency again upon what she perceives to be a strong, powerful, aggressive, controlling advocate who will leave her still dependent, never having learned that she has power and the ability to grow and change and become independent of abusive relationships.

All of this will not occur in mediation, either; but as part of the mediation of cases in which there is spousal abuse, she will be required to participate in counseling that will help her learn the reasons for her entering into such a relationship and will assist her in learning new behaviors and strengths that will empower her beyond the criteria of being the victim. In mediation she will learn to speak for herself and be heard and respected. She will also learn about all of the assets and liabilities and have her questions answered. In my opinion, the combination of therapy and mediation is most therapeutic and healthy for any couple facing divorce.

Ron and Sue concluded mediation with a settlement based upon their standards of fairness unique to their facts and interests. All in all, it was not unlike other settlements I have mediated. However, the process was more intense.

5

Parenting Disputes: Who Will Have the Children?

Bill and Charlene Curtis were married in their mid-twenties. They have one child, Terri, age 11. They attended the first mediation session on referral from their attorneys, who had suggested mediation due to the fact that the couple could not afford the $20,000.000 needed to properly conduct a custody trial.

Both were represented by attorneys known for their skill at litigating. In addition, their attorneys are also expensive and, as is sometimes the case when clients get behind in their bills and cannot pay the necessary upfront money to hire the expert witnesses (i.e., child psychologists, etc.) while also paying the ongoing costs of litigation, the attorneys will suggest mediation to their clients. (Some attorneys will always suggest mediation to resolve a custody dispute.) In those cases where there has been extensive litigation, the attorneys who are particularly litigious will often recommend mediation rather than withdrawing from the case because the client cannot pay the fees. I suspect this was the case with Charlene and Bill, because both of them told me that they had bills in excess of $5,000.00 dollars that had not been paid to their attorneys. This was in addition to the $4,000.000–$6,000.00 that each of them had already paid to an attorney throughout the course of the litigation since their separation eleven months earlier.

For the past 18 months they had been living apart. Subsequent to the filing of a petition for dissolution of the marriage a year earlier, they returned to court four times on various motions relating to support. The first court appearance at the time the petition for dissolution was filed granted temporary physical custody of the minor child to Charlene, and Bill was given three weeks to "vacate the premises." Bill has been living in an apartment about 20 minutes from the family home, but in another school district.

INTAKE PROCEDURE

At the orientation session, I started by asking what the largest issue was for each. Bill spoke first, saying, "The biggest issue for me is who will have Terri." I turned to Charlene and asked the same question. Her response was similar. She said that they were scheduled to have a custody trial in two months and their attorneys had suggested mediation as a possible way of settling the matter.

Because I use the orientation session to lay the ground-

work for changing some attitudes, I responded immediately by saying, "You know, I really don't think it is a
question of who will have the children. In my opinion, it
is rather a question of *when* each of you will have the
children."

Leading both of them on, I said to Charlene, "You are-
n't trying to terminate his parental rights are you?" to
which she replied with the anticipated, "No, I've never
prevented him from seeing Terri." I then turned to Bill
and asked the same question. He replied, "Of course not,
but. . . ." I interrupted him and said, "Good! Because if
either one of you had indicated to me that you were trying
to terminate the parental rights of the other, I would have
to stop our orientation session and say right now that I
could not go any further and become your mediator. The
reason is that I am unable to mediate custody. Fighting
over custody means that the two of you are presenting
evidence about who was a better or worse parent in the
past to determine a higher or lower level of ownership. I
am not interested in asking the two of you the question
of who will own the children; I am interested in asking
you this question: What are the future parenting arrangements the two of you can agree to so that each of you
can become the good, loving parents you wish to be, even
though you are living apart?"

At this point, approximately five minutes into my first
session with them, I proceeded to tell them about my role.
"I want to use our first session to accomplish three things.
First, I believe that if any couple is going to hire a professional to help them, be it a therapist, an attorney or a
doctor, but particularly a mediator who is by definition
neutral and unbiased, they need an opportunity to meet
that person and determine whether they feel comfortable
and trusting of that person. Second, even though people

may have heard of mediation through its greater use and read reports about it in the news media, I still need an opportunity to explain in some detail exactly what it is I do in this room and how I go about helping the two of you reach agreement. Third, I want to find out about some of your own special issues and concerns so I can explain how we would go about resolving those issues in mediation."

By stating these three goals for the orientation session, I have accomplished several objectives. I have first of all gained control of the meeting and made very clear who is in charge of the session. Second, I have promised them that I will explain the process of mediation, but will not necessarily promise to settle any issues at the first meeting. Third, by engaging them in discussion about the custody issue for them, I have already started to implement one of my roles as a mediator, which is to redefine the disputes in a more mutual, less adversarial fashion.

I continued with the following explanation. "I understand that this may be a very difficult time for both of you. First of all let me point out that through all of this, my role is not to make decisions for you, but rather to participate in your discussions in such away as to make it easy for you to make these decisions yourself."

Charlene interrupted at this point and said, "I really don't think this will work and I am here only because I agreed to come. I really can't trust anything he does and even if we do agree to anything, it won't work because he never keeps his agreements." Bill responded to this, in an obviously tense voice, "You're the one who never keeps your agreements. I can't even have a weekend with Terri that you don't screw up." (I didn't want to interrupt Bill this time, because I had already interrupted him once and if he were to get the idea that I was not balanced in my management of the communications, he might not trust me as the mediator.) He continued by yelling that if Terri were given a choice about where to live, she would choose her father.

I tried to take back control of the discussion by pointing out that the state of Ohio has for many years had a minor preference law that allows children to choose, at age 12, with whom they wish to live. "That law has caused countless distressing problems, because as soon as the children approach age 12, they start to threaten the parent they are living with by saying that if they can't have their way, they will choose to live with the other parent."

I suggested that they not leave the problem in Terri's hands, but rather take control of the situation by deciding to resolve the problem themselves. "There are really only two choices," I continued, "You can decide yourselves or a judge will decide for you. My experience as a mediator and as an attorney has been that people would rather decide for themselves and I suspect that is why both of you came here today."

Sensing that they were both frustrated, I asked, "Do either of you have some fear that you will not be able to be successful in mediation?" I looked at Bill and said, "I'll start with you first."

Bill was very direct. He said, "Since we have been apart, my wife (I interrupted at this point and asked him to refer to his wife as Charlene) has dragged me back into court three times, always asking for more money. I don't think she would agree to anything unless it took everything I had and even then she would not be satisfied."

I responded by saying that I thought they were here to discuss custody and it appears that money will also be a concern. I pointed out that I frequently find that battles

over custody are also battles around money. The reason
they become battles about money is that our child support guidelines call for money to be paid by the parent
who loses custody to the parent who wins custody. "While
I am not trying to suggest that either of you are concerned only about money and not about your daughter,
we will have to make sure that whatever fair agreements
are reached are also fair agreements concerning money."

Charlene said she wanted to respond to my question
about fears. She has fears that anytime she says anything
to Bill about Terri, it will appear in an affidavit against
her. She didn't think she even wanted to be in the same
room with him because he always twists around everything she says. I responded by saying: "First of all, you
only have to fear his affidavits if you get into court again.
I believe that the reason both of you have been continually going back and forth in court is that you have not
been getting your needs met. As soon as you start getting
your needs met, you will not have any purpose or reason
for going to court. And if you never have to appear in
court again because you have settled things yourselves,
you don't have to worry about anything coming back
against you."

At this point, I was trying to reduce some of their pain
by laying blame for it not on them, but on the adversarial
system they had been using to solve their problems.

I further pointed out that most people who begin mediation are not quite as sure as I am about their ability to
stay out of court. For that reason, it is necessary to make
sure that whatever is said in the mediation room does not
get used against either in court. At this point I provided
them with copies of the rules (see Appendix A) and asked
them to look at the section on confidentiality of the mediation discussions. I stressed that should they decide to

begin mediation with me as their mediator they would be required to sign a binding written Agreement to Begin Mediation (see Appendix B) which requires them to adopt all of the rules, including the rule about privacy and confidentiality of the mediation discussions. I would not be required to appear in court as a witness to testify or give opinions about who was a better or worse parent. Moreover, since these are settlement discussions, and since the rules specifically prohibit them from using testimony obtained in mediation, neither of them would be able to use statements made in mediation. I stressed that it is absolutely essential that they be able to hold open and honest discussions in mediation without having to fear that whatever they say might later come back to be used against them in some way.

Finally, as if to give another bit of assurance, I indicated that, if they wish, I would ask their attorneys to also sign the Agreement to Begin Mediation, thus witnessing their commitment to this rule of the process.

At this point, I began to cover some issues about fees and my estimation about time to complete the mediation process. Both seemed willing at this point to allow me to complete some of the housekeeping matters and I was somewhat surprised that they did not get into a disagreement about fees. Both agreed to share the fees equally and I finally got around to asking a question that I normally ask earlier in the first one-hour meeting. I wanted to know what they were now doing as far as a schedule for the exchange of Terri.

The response from both of them was predictable in the sense that most couples who are in a great deal of conflict around the custody issue frequently have problems because they have no rules. Bill said they were not really following a schedule due to the fact that his business frequently required him to be out of town and it was not always possible to know in advance what his commitments were. He also said that he wanted to be able to drop in any time and see Terri. Charlene said she has never prevented him from seeing Terri any time he wants. He simply has to remember that Terri is very busy and has her own schedule and it's not fair to make Terri see him if she has school activities and other commitments.

At this point I said in a gentle voice: "If you want to make progress toward settlement, the first thing I want to do is help you establish a schedule for the exchange of Terri. It doesn't matter whether Terri lives with Mom or Dad, if you don't have a schedule, there is chaos." Charlene did say at this point that a schedule would at least require him to follow through on his commitments to be with Terri. I turned to Bob and was about to speak when he said that he didn't want to be tied down to a schedule. I tried to assure him that no schedule is going to be completely inflexible, but that establishment of a schedule is about the only thing that works to answer so many of the questions and problems over parenting in separate houses. I listed and explained several of the improvements that are accomplished by a schedule:

1. Terri will have a commitment from the parent out of the home that there will be regular, recurring contact.
2. The parent in the home, in this case Mom, will now be able to plan her own time and will be able to count on time off from the duties of parenting.
3. There will no longer be a need for Dad to make seven or eight phone calls to Terri or Mom in order to establish one visit.

4. There will be less contact between Mom and Dad because a weekly recurring schedule does not require so
   much effort to implement. It implements itself.
5. There will be fewer disappointments over last-minute
   requests from Dad to spend time with Terri only to
   learn that she has already made other plans.

Both parents indicated that some of the problems addressed by the above have been and were continuing to
occur. Bill pointed out that he still didn't think he would
be able to spend as much time as he wanted with Terri
because her mother had her involved in so many activities that there was no time left to be with Dad.

I responded to this by observing that Bill cannot get his
needs as a parent met without the help of Charlene and
Charlene cannot get her needs as a parent met without
the help of Bill. First of all, there really isn't any problem
concerning the school and church activities of Terri. She
can just as well do them from Dad's place as well as from
the original family home where she and Mom live most
of the time. In addition, it might be necessary for Mom
to encourage Terri to be with her Dad after they agreed
to a schedule.

Charlene stated at this point that she frequently has to
make Terri go with her Dad even though she doesn't want
to go and would rather be with her friends on the weekend. I turned to Bill and asked him whether he was aware
of the fact that Charlene would encourage Terri to spend
time with her father even though she might be reluctant.
My hope at this point was to find something that showed
there was even the slightest fragment of caring and cooperative behavior still occurring. My hopes were dashed

when Bill said, "She only says things like that to impress you. I know she really doesn't want Terri to be with me."

At this point the hour was almost over and I asked both of them if what I said was making any sense to them. Charlene spoke first and indicated that the psychologist the entire family had seen stressed that they needed to end the warfare between the two of them and she said she would be willing to give it a try. Bill then spoke and said he had always been willing to settle things and in fact had asked her to consider mediation before they ever got involved with attorneys. I concluded the consultation session by scheduling a first working session for the following week. I gave them each questionnaires (see Appendix C) to fill out independently and asked each of them to read the book, *Mom's House, Dad's House* (Ricci, 1980).

PROCESS USED TO ANALYZE THE CASE

As mentioned elsewhere in Chapter 3, it is not necessary to analyze the case from the viewpoint of a therapist or psychologist taking a family history of the conflict in order to then devise a treatment strategy. Such an approach would require too much time and would likely divert attention from my goal for the first meeting or initial interview. In addition, it would unduly emphasize the past, which for most couples is painful and needs changing, not highlighting. Therefore, I have found it most useful to learn what is necessary about the past through an interchange with the couple that allows me to explain the mediation process in an organized fashion. By listening carefully to their responses and concerns, I can usually learn all that is needed to go forward with my intervention. Indeed, since the interventions used are basic with almost every couple, it is not really necessary to have a complete family conflict history in order to commence the "treatment" plan.

I learned this principle from one of the earliest custody cases I experienced. One of the first couples referred to me for custody mediation brought a huge manila envelope to my office which contained the entire custody investigation file of the court services custody investigation unit. The couple spent the first three hours of mediation arguing about inaccuracies contained in the various reports and we did not begin to make progress towards the settlement until I insisted the custody investigation file be put away and not discussed again until I decided it was necessary. We finally settled the custody dispute in two more sessions without ever reviewing the file again. (Although many of the concerns expressed in the custody investigation report were addressed in mediation, I learned that it wastes valuable time to rehash the past because none of us have the power the change the past. We can possibly control only some of the future.)

During the initial consultation, I try to accomplish three main goals. These goals are to (1) form a relationship with the couple, (2) educate them about the process, methods and goals of mediation, and (3) set the stage for cooperation to begin. After touching on all three of these areas in a one-hour consultation, I will then ask them to make a commitment to begin mediation. Several techniques are used to form a relationship with the couple. Many of the techniques are familiar to therapists and psychologists who must also form a relationship with the clients they are to help. However, in the role of the mediator, one must remember that different methods are used because the role of the mediator is different from the role of the therapist. These methods are summarized as follows:

1. **Be neutral:** It is important to assure both husband and wife that the mediator is neutral and unbiased. The couple will be looking for certain clues that the mediator favors one person over the other. The mediation process will not be successful if one of the parties believes, either correctly or incorrectly, that the mediator is siding with the other. This can be accomplished by equal eye contact and positioning oneself approximately equidistant from each of them. In addition, it is necessary for the mediator to become proficient at developing a way of answering the couple's questions and concerns without showing evidence of bias or favoritism. The best technique is a factual response that focuses the answer to their question back on their mutual shoulders.

2. **Be honest:** By the time couples arrive at the mediation table, they may not trust their attorneys or themselves. They certainly may have lost trust in their soon-to-be-ex-marriage partner. By responding directly and honestly to each question, the mediator begins to gain some trust from each of them.

3. **Validate their concerns:** Prior to entering mediation, the family lives of most couples in conflict have been marked by failure and frustration. Their attorneys may have told them of the vagaries and risks in the divorce process. They have friends and relatives telling them to prepare for the worst and to get the best, meanest attorney in town because the battle will be long and

hard. Then, as if everything else isn't enough, they find themselves engaged in a battle over their most prized possession, the thing that is in many cases their reason for living—their child. Any concern that is expressed by either the wife or the husband should be taken seriously and hope must be created that there is always a way to find an answer to any concern.

4. **Establish control:** Couples are looking for professional assistance and will respect a mediator who takes charge of the discussions and keeps the mediation room a safe environment. In the case of Charlene and Bill, there certainly were instances where they might not have liked being interrupted, but there was no doubt at the end of one hour who was in charge of the discussions. Such exercise of control assures them that the sessions will not become emotionally violent or unsafe and it also gives them the impression that perhaps the mediator can in fact help.

If divorcing couples are going to be successful in mediation, they have to know what to expect and they must be clear on the goals of the process. At each initial session, most of the following points are addressed:

1. **Steps and process:** Although every case is different, there will be several steps that must be completed before a final parenting agreement can be accepted by both. These steps involve getting agreement on facts and needs, and then looking at a range of options before selecting one or more choices.

2. **Role of the mediator:** As the couple become more aware that the role of the mediator is not to make decisions for them, but to forcefully help them go about getting

to agreement through a different method than they have experienced, they occasionally feel a sense of empowerment. It is too early for Bill and Charlene to understand what this means. They are still in the stage of complaining about the other, but they will soon learn exactly what was meant by the statement that they are in the soup together and each needs the assistance of the other in order to continue to be the good, loving parents they wish to be. Because the role of the mediator is not one that many people are familiar with, it is often necessary to explain this phase of the process by example, that is, by occasionally intervening with the statement that something is or is not part of my role as mediator.

3. **Role of attorneys, experts and the court system:** In an initial consultation, it can be helpful to discuss the other players in the process. Couples are told that it may be necessary to obtain the assistance of an expert, such as a child psychologist, not for the purpose of custody investigation, but to assist Mom and Dad as a neutral expert should questions of the children's behavior become an issue. Additionally, since all couples in mediation will eventually need to have the agreements reached in mediation reviewed and implemented by attorneys of their own choice, it is necessary to explain the cooperative relationship between mediation and the attorneys who implement the decisions of the couple.

4. **Discuss the rules and guidelines:** With Bill and Charlene, I found it necessary to explain in detail the rule about confidentiality of the mediation process because Charlene was fearful that her statements made in mediation would ultimately be used against her. In order to counter the criticism by many in the legal profes-

sion that mediation is "loosey-goosey," the rules serve
the purpose of adding written structure to the process.
I was successful in countering their fears about confidentiality because they agreed to return for a first
working session. I also informed them that the rules
prohibited either of them from ever calling me as a
witness in the unlikely event they reached an impasse.
I specifically assured them that because of the rules, I
have never been called upon to tell a court who I
thought was a better or worse parent. Therefore, they
should be able to have a high degree of certainty that
this would not happen to them.

5. **Discuss the goals of mediation:** With Charlene and Bill,
I pointed out that the primary goal of mediation is to
achieve a detailed written agreement that will serve as
the settlement and will be adopted as a part of their
Judgment and Decree of Dissolution. With both of
them, I stressed the obvious benefits of resolving their
current dispute. This discussion must have had some
impact on Charlene because she remarked that their
psychologist had urged them to end the fighting for
the sake of Terri.

If the couple are going to be successful in mediation,
they will accomplish this goal only when they find reasons for beginning to cooperate. Therefore, much of my
effort during the initial session is directed towards setting
the stage for cooperation to occur. Although I am not able
to construct an entire stage with every couple in the one-
hour initial consult, the following concepts were to a
greater or lesser degree touched upon in my first meeting
with Charlene and Bill:

1. **Mutuality:** I try never to miss an opportunity to remind the couple that they are in the soup together and can achieve fair results only by attacking problems rather than each other. This was stressed with Bill and Charlene when I pointed out that neither of them could get their needs met as parents without the help of the other. The technique used to accomplish this is similar in a way to what I attempted to accomplish as an attorney in a custody trial. Whereas I would always listen very closely to the testimony of an adverse witness in order to catch that witness in a statement of bias, ambiguity or inconsistency, I no longer listen for differences. I now try to listen closely for statements that emphasize the connectedness of the couple. As a mediator, I make a conscious effort to reinforce any evidence of cooperative behavior and tend to minimize and normalize evidence of negative and conflicted behavior.

2. **Stress the future rather than the past:** I also pointed out to Bill and Charlene that I did not have the power to help them change the past (no matter how bad it might have been), but I do have the power to help them shape the future in a way that is fair to both of them. At one point, I asked both where Terri would be for Christmas. Each replied that it has not yet been agreed to and their attorneys were supposed to be negotiating that issue through letters. Seizing the opportunity, I said, "It would be better if both of you could talk about that right now."

   It turned out that the main roadblock was Bill's request to take Terri to Chicago to spend some time at Christmas with his parents. Charlene objected on the grounds that she would not give up Christmas in or-

der for him to take Terri to Chicago. Bill then said in
a frustrated voice that he only wanted to take her there
for a weekend and it didn't have to interfere with
Christmas Eve or Christmas Day, it could be the weekend before or the weekend after. Just when I thought
we might have a breakthrough, Charlene said that even
if they split Christmas Eve and Christmas Day, and
each has Terri for one of them, she would have to think
more about when she would let him take Terri, if at
all.

Without sharing my conclusion, I made a note to
myself that another issue to be addressed in the working sessions concerned the issue of control and power.
I anticipated the need to spend some time in the next
working session on helping them address the issue of
learning a more cooperative method of sharing Terri,
rather than Bill always feeling he would need to come
to Charlene and beg for time with Terri, only to hear
that she would think about it and let him know. I ended
this discussion by remarking, "The beauty of having a
schedule is that it gets both of you out of the game of
fighting for power each time an exception to the regular schedule might be needed, as in the case of holidays and other special events."

The initial session concluded with Charlene and Bill
making an appointment for the following Monday. I made
several notes to myself after they left indicating a concern
about power and control, but still not really knowing what
lay at the root of their animosity and bitterness towards
each other. I made a further note to myself to explore the
issue of the emotional divorce. I suspected that one of
them, perhaps Bill, may still not be accepting of the fact

that a divorce was occurring. Although I frequently ask at the initial session whether both of them are in agreement that the marriage should end, I had not asked this question of them during my first one hour.

CONCEPTUAL FRAMEWORK USED TO MEDIATE CASE

With Charlene and Bill, I was convinced that I would make no progress unless I was able to end the first working session with some small written agreements. At a minimum, I wanted to get in writing an agreed-to weekly schedule of exchanges and the beginning of a holiday schedule, essential with Christmas only two months away. In addition, I felt that it was necessary for them to begin to understand exactly what they disagreed about. I would not let them simply say they disagree about who should have custody.

When they returned the following Monday, Charlene was 15 minutes late and Bill was visibly upset. I ignored his anger and immediately stood up and moved beside the flip chart, marking pen in hand.

I asked, "What schedule for the exchange of Terri are you now following?" As I asked this question, I constructed a large square and proceeded to break it into 28 separate squares (see p. 134).

Charlene said the court had ordered every other weekend and every Wednesday evening visitation by Bill. At this point, I put the flip chart pen back into my pocket and sat down. Turning to both of them, I said, "I think we will have a better chance of getting agreement if we use different words. You both remember that I said to Bill at our initial session last week that I preferred the two of you not use the word 'custody.' Now I am also going to

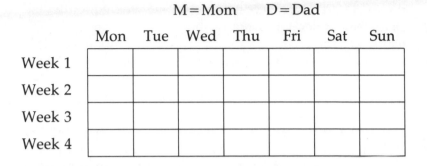

ask that you not use the word 'visitation.' My reason for this is that I think both of you are going to have to parent your children. When I was a teenager, I used to have to go up north and visit my cousins in the summer. If I were divorced, I would not want to visit my children; I think I would rather parent them."

I asked if this made any sense and whether they agreed with me. Bill spoke first, saying, "All I want is 50/50 time sharing. In fact, all I really want is for her to stop trying to take Terri from me."

"What do you mean by the words 'take Terri from me'?" I asked him.

Bill responded, "I mean that as soon as she gets custody, she will be free to move wherever she wants and she has already said she plans to move to Los Angeles."

At this point, Charlene interrupted and said, "You know for a fact that we moved from the West Coast to this god-forsaken tundra only so you could advance your career."

As is almost always the case in custody mediation, the battle for control of the child or children is never really over the children. It is directly related to something else—usually money, a planned move out of state, or simply the attorney's advice that becoming designated as the "custodial" parent or the parent having "physical custody" means the winner is in a better position should future court appearances be required after the divorce.

I proceeded to tell them that neither may ever permanently remove their child from the state without the written permission of the other or the consent of the court. I did acknowledge that their attorneys were correct in pointing out that whoever is designed as having "physical custody" does have the edge in future court appearances should either want to move from the state and take Terri along. I assured them that there were several mechanisms they could use to deal with such a problem.

I wanted to get back to the weekly schedule because it was apparent they were doing a good job of sidetracking me, but before returning to the blank flip chart, I wanted to comment more about the out-of-state move.

"Do either of you have any immediate, concrete plans to move to another state?" Both answered no.

I continued, "My experience has been that most couples are able to very satisfactorily agree on out-of-state move arrangements provided they have built up a history of making the weekly exchanges and the in-state parenting work. You two have had a difficult time exchanging Terri between your two homes and you don't live more than 20 minutes apart. Why don't we try to work on the weekly schedule."

Turning the flip chart, I reminded them about their earlier statement that they were not following any schedule. I remarked how that seemed strange, because they have been to court several times and didn't the judge enter a temporary order setting out a temporary schedule? Well, it turned out the judge had indeed ordered the standard every other weekend and Wednesday evening to occur on a temporary basis, but they were not following it. I asked why they were not following it.

Charlene indicated that the temporary schedule in the court papers was not being followed because of Bill's unpredictable travel schedule and because he is the volunteer basketball coach for the girl's community athletic association. Terri was very athletic and I learned that as soon as basketball was over, swimming would start and Dad was one of the volunteer assistant coaches. I sat down and then said, "Now let me guess, in the summer is it soccer or girl's softball?" Bill spoke up, saying that he and Terri had just had a talk about that and Terri has decided to be on the girl's softball team. Bill added that he had stopped by the YWCA that very morning to sign up as a volunteer coach for the summer softball program.

When I inquired about the current schedule for girl's basketball, Charlene angrily said, "He went and signed her on with the traveling squad and they play every weekend, all winter." As we talked further, the picture that emerged was one of almost constant contact by Bill, but following no regular or recurring schedule, only following the athletic schedule of games and practices, as well as whenever Bill decided he wanted to drop by the house and spend time with Terri.

I said in a thoughtful voice, "It looks as if Bill, even though he is technically the temporary noncustodial parent, has contact with Terri as much time as, if not more than, Mom, considering that both of you work and Terri is in school each day." At this point, Bill proudly announced that he has seen Terri 22 out of the last 30 days. Charlene exploded, as I had expected. She was quite vituperative. She started with an attack on Bill for keeping his journal, to which Bill defensively responded that he was doing it only because his attorney asked him to keep track of his contact. Charlene then proceeded to point out that she had been very liberal in allowing Bill to see Terri as much as he wanted, even though her attorney had told her she was wrong to be so nice to him. I interrupted Charlene and asked when she managed to have any time by herself with Terri and Charlene responded that when she and Terri did try to plan something, Bill would screw it up by figuring out some reason he had to be with Terri.

Over the past several months, as this crazy cycle got more and more out of control, Charlene would occasionally put her foot down and resist Bill's plans, only to end in wild and threatening arguments carried out on the front porch. "Do you see what must be happening to Terri?" I said. "She certainly must love both of you, but the constant tugging for her time and attention must be an awful burden on her." (Bill would first make his plans with Terri and then when he appeared at the house to pick her up, Charlene would be put in a position where she had to say yes to the contact.)

"Could it be any other way for the two of you? You each think the other is trying to take Terri away from you. As Dad finds more and more ways for Terri to be involved with him, Mom feels that her life becomes more and more invaded by Dad. It is absolutely essential that the two of you start to follow a schedule, otherwise Charlene will fight to the bitter end to obtain a custody ruling in her favor in order to establish some control over her life again. Do you see that, Bill? And, in addition, whenever Mom tries to say no to Dad's continual involvement with Terri, Dad interprets that as interference in his relationship with Terri. Both of you think that by winning a custody trial, you will be able to get your needs met. Let

me tell you something I fear neither of you will understand right now: A custody ruling in favor of one of you
is not the answer to your problems; it would be only the
beginning of even worse problems. The only way to stop
the chaos and get both of your needs met is to establish
a schedule the two of you will rigidly adhere to for a time,
and I guarantee that this will get things back to normal.''

Turning to Charlene, I asked her to help me to construct a schedule that she would find acceptable. She said
what the court ordered at the temporary hearing was just
fine with her. I filled in the blanks and said, ''Is this what
it would look like?'' She nodded her head, yes.

As I turned to speak to Bill, he blurted out, ''That's
outrageous!''

I asked, ''What schedule would you not find outrageous?'' He said he wanted equal 50/50 time sharing and
nothing less than that would do.

I asked, ''Why do you want equal time-sharing?''

''Because it's fair,'' Bill said.

I continued, ''Why is that fair?''

''Because I'm just as good a parent as she is.''

''Bill,'' I said, ''We're not talking today about who is a
better or worse parent.'' Turning to Charlene, I asked her

M = Mom   D = Dad

	Mon	Tue	Wed	Thu	Fri	Sat	Sun
Week 1	M	M	M/D	M	M/D	D	D
Week 2	M	M	M/D	M	M	M	M
Week 3	M	M	M/D	M	M/D	D	D
Week 4	M	M	M/D	M	M	M	M

if she would be willing to agree to a 50/50 time-sharing. She responded with an "Absolutely not."

I asked Bill what type of 50/50 sharing arrangement he would propose and he said, "Six months with me and six months with her mother." I wondered aloud whether or not that would work very well with him living in an apartment outside of the school district. Bill then said, "If she would stop fighting me every inch of the way, I would then have some money to move into a house in the school district."

I mentioned to both of them that very few people who ultimately choose equal time-sharing follow a six months on and six months off schedule. In fact, I told them that in working as a professional divorce mediator the past 11 years, I have not had one couple who chose to divide the year in half. Many choose every other week or every two week exchanges and I think the reason is that six months of primary parenting and six months of being the secondary parent are too long for both sides of the coin.

The two-hour session was nearing an end and I asked them if they would agree to meet with me on Friday. I assigned Bill the task of obtaining the rest of the traveling basketball schedule and I asked Charlene to get the school schedule for the rest of the year and bring it to Friday's session.

ROADBLOCKS

Throughout the remainder of the next three two-hour sessions, the critical issues that served as roadblocks to a settlement were:

1. The absence of a recurring weekly schedule that would establish boundaries, especially for Charlene.

2. The dispute over 50/50 time-sharing as opposed to every other weekend and Wednesday evening "visitations" by Bill.
3. The continuing dispute over who controlled Terri's time. Was it left for Charlene to decide when Dad would be given extra time with Terri (because she was granted temporary custody) or was it Bill's right to drop in any time he wished?
4. The concern expressed by Bill about Charlene and Terri moving to another state after the custody trial.

STRATEGIES USED TO PROMOTE SETTLEMENT

At the third working session, I decided to again focus on completing the weekly schedule because I felt such a schedule would establish boundaries and reduce the power dispute concerning who has veto power over the schedule. A breakthrough was achieved when I asked them if they could agree to try a schedule for only a two-month period. Knowing that Bill still wanted 50/50 time-sharing, I asked them both to agree that at the end of two months, if one or both did not like the way it worked, we would go back to the present situation, which was essentially no schedule. Near the end of the third two-hour session, we had reviewed the winter basketball schedule and also learned that Bill really can control his own schedule of business travel because he was part owner of the business.

Charlene brought the school calendar and, to obtain a settlement, I compromised my own goal of getting a recurring schedule that worked for any month of the year by constructing a 60-day grid with the actual calendar days placed in the corner of each square. By the end of the third two-hour session, they had completed a schedule for the next 60 days which called for alternating weekends and at least two, occasionally three, evenings of contact each week by Bill. As a precaution, I suggested that they agree to the concept of the "on-duty/off-duty" parent as a mechanism for dealing with exceptions to the 60-day schedule. We reviewed the following language and I explained that many couples follow this procedure:

> Husband and Wife agree to the concept of allowing each to provide parenting during the times they are scheduled to care for the children. This means that if the children are ill or Husband or Wife have other obligations during the scheduled time with the children, it will be the responsibility of the on-duty parent to care for the children. Both welcome the on-duty parent to request assistance during their scheduled times with the children, but both Wife and Husband understand that if the off-duty parent is not able to assist the on-duty parent during the scheduled times with the children, it will be the responsibility of the on-duty parent to make alternative arrangements for the children.

This language basically provides a mechanism for each to ask the other to change the schedule. In most cases, such a request is acceptable. However, if one has made plans and cannot accommodate the other, that parent is free to decline the request (without feeling guilty) and then the scheduled parent is on-duty (or off-duty) and the schedule must be followed.

I sold them on this notion primarily because both wanted to eliminate the constant power plays, while at the same time trusting my claim that the situation would improve if they adopted some rules. Bill was still more resistant to the need for a schedule, but finally agreed when Charlene said she would consider selling the house and splitting the equity so that they could both live in the same school district.

I decided to schedule the next working session in one month, telling Charlene and Bill that I wanted them to practice the next four weeks at making the schedule work. When they returned, I began by asking them how the schedule was going. Charlene said it was an improvement. Surprisingly, Bill agreed that it was working. The discussion took a decidedly hostile course when Charlene raised a complaint about Bill entering the house without her permission. It seems that Bill brought Terri back on Sunday afternoon and, seeing that Charlene was gone, went in the side door and made two long-distance phone calls, leaving some money on the kitchen counter. This incident required another discussion about boundaries, which finally resulted in Bill agreeing to return the garage opener, even though he no longer had keys to the house.

I observed that one reason people get into scrapes about keys and boundaries is they have not yet finished the business of the emotional divorce. Through further questioning, I learned they had not received any counseling concerning the breakup of the marriage. In fact, Bill said, "I still don't know why she wants to divorce me." I presented my opinion that one of the underlying reasons they were having such a fight over custody was due to some unfinished emotional business of ending the marriage relationship.

At first, Charlene resisted my suggestion that they both attend one or two joint sessions with a therapist I would recommend. I was able to obtain her agreement to attend at least one joint session when I told her that the work in

a therapy session would help Bill "let go" of the relationship and he would therefore be less likely to invade her
boundaries. Bill, of course, liked the idea of getting her
to a joint counseling session because he still held to the
fantasy that the marriage could be saved. I told Bill that
my purpose in making the referral was to help him understand and accept the reasons for their divorce.

Since there was still one hour left of the session, I focused on the out-of-state move question. I opened this
discussion by asking them to explain for me how the possibility of such a move affects their present negotiations.
Charlene started by saying all of her family lives elsewhere and she was not happy with her current position
as an insurance company risk management specialist. She
wanted to leave open the option of moving and she as-
sumed Terri would probably move with her. She admitted she had no concrete offers elsewhere and she did acknowledge that she wanted to be designated "physical
custodian" of Terri on the advice of her attorney.

I pointed out that even if she is granted physical custody by the court or by agreement with Bill, she could
not remove Terri from the state without consent of Bill or
permission of the court. After hearing Bill's fears about
her wanting to take Terri from him, I said: "First of all, I
don't hear anything that says Charlene has plans to immediately move from the state after the divorce is entered
and she knows she must first obtain your approval. Now,
it is true that the person designated as having physical
custody is in a slightly better position should you wind
up before a judge two years from now arguing about an
out-of-state move. The reason for the edge is that the legal burden of proof is greater for the parent not designated physical custodian. However, the custody labels will
never be important if you avoid court in the future. There

are several options you might wish to consider that would help defuse this issue. First, Terri is in the 7th grade and I believe she changes school and will be attending senior high beginning in the tenth grade. Could you both agree to commit yourselves to remaining in the state for at least the next two and one half years? You don't have to answer this question now. Second, it is seldom possible to negotiate today the exact terms of an out-of-state parenting agreement because you have not had sufficient time to make the current arrangements work successfully. No matter what choices you make now, you cannot settle this particular issue at this time. Rather, you can agree on a mechanism you will follow in the future to solve any potential move in a fair way. Instead of hoping that the choice of custody labels will solve this problem for you, why not consider a binding arbitration clause in your Decree that would require any future dispute to be settled by arbitration? The arbitrators are chosen from a panel of mental health experts and I believe that the arbitrators, because of their background, will not rely on what label was chosen in 1987 to guide them, but rather will try to decide the issue on the circumstances as they really are in the future."

The following Binding Arbitration clause was discussed at this point:

Should they have any major parenting disputes in the future that cannot be resolved after making a good faith effort in mediation, they agree to submit the parenting dispute to binding arbitration. The arbitrators will be chosen from a panel maintained by ERICKSON MEDIATION INSTITUTE and the arbitrators will consist of three mental health professionals who will have the right to interview the minor children as well as the parents. The arbitration hearing will be subject to the terms and conditions of the Minnesota Arbitration Act and Rules of Arbitration for Parenting Disputes published by ERICKSON MEDIATION INSTITUTE and in effect at the time the arbitration is commenced. Both Husband and Wife understand that by agreeing to binding arbitration, they may not have the dispute heard in a District Court and the ruling of the arbitrators is final and not subject to review except under certain narrow conditions.

After further discussion, both agreed that arbitration would be an acceptable method of resolving the out-of-state move. They did not wish to agree to the two and one-half year limitation on staying in the state. I was surprised and I finally concluded that both were so weary of their previous court appearances that they would choose anything to keep from having to go through more court hearings. Charlene said it made sense to have a mental health expert, rather than some judge, decide future parenting disputes. Bill was only too happy to agree as he felt he had not been treated fairly in previous court appearances.

SUMMARY

The final settlement was obtained at the fourth session when Charlene agreed to place their homestead on the market for sale and divide the equity equally with Bill. This permitted him to start looking for a home in the same school district. Charlene did not agree to 50/50 time-sharing, but did agree to a clause in their decree that called for a review of the schedule 12 months after the entry of decree. She said she would consider 50/50 time-sharing at that time if Bill respected her boundaries. They agreed to joint legal and joint physical custody, with the binding arbitration clause.

The roadblocks to settlement were successfully removed through a combination of strategies. The three joint counseling sessions helped Bill to recognize the need to honor Charlene's boundaries. The therapist asked that Terri attend the third session and her statements at this meeting helped Charlene realize the important role Dad played in Charlene's life. This led, I believe, to Charlene's willingness to consider 50/50 time-sharing. The adoption of the binding arbitration clause removed the significance of the custody labels and the adoption of a regular weekly schedule ended most of the power struggles, as I predicted it would. Charlene and Bill were still experiencing frequent contact about exceptions to the schedule and I pointed out my concern to them that the requests for changes must not always come from Bill. While he promised to try to follow the schedule as religiously as possible, he basically seemed to be an unstructured person who will always resist rigid rules.

Their final settlement allowed them to avoid the need for a custody trial where each would have to present evidence about the other parent's bad conduct. It also eliminated the need for Bill to keep a record of the number of contacts he made with Terri each month. Terri has stopped seeing the psychologist and she decided to skip organized sports in the summer. Charlene sent a Christmas card to our office two years ago and I have not heard from either of them since the final mediation session.

6

Maternal Grandparents and Dad: Who Will Raise Christine?

The case of Christine, age 10 months, was not only a potential child protection case, but also contained the elements of a nasty custody battle between generations and possibly over state lines. Christine was born out of wedlock and shortly afterwards her mother died in a tragic accident. Relatives of the deceased mother consulted an attorney and soon, the maternal grandparents (Joanne and Bob) and the maternal aunt and uncle (Sara and Steve) were lined up against the natural father (John). Three mediation sessions over a period of six months eventually led to resolution at the final session when John's father decided to attend. Each session was approximately two hours in length.

INITIAL CONTACT

For several months after the death of the mother, her sister and parents provided care for Christine. The case was referred to Family Mediation Services by their attorney who believed this type of problem would be best served by mediation. The legal issues were unclear and both sides faced some risk in court due to the fact that the natural father had actually provided less care for Christine since the mother's death. Christine's mother, Karen, had been living with Christine's father at the time of her death, although they had never married. John lived in a small rural town about 70 miles from the maternal extended family. Since Karen's death, John had been bringing Christine to Joanne and Bob's every Sunday through Friday while he worked. Christine lived with Joanne and Bob during the week and went to Sara's each day while Joanne worked. Sara had been very close to Karen and enjoyed caring for Christine.

The initial problem, as explained by Joanne, was that John did not follow through on his promise to pay Christine's expenses incurred by Joanne and Sara. John had promised to turn over the social security checks, plus an additional $30.00 per week to Sara and Joanne. However, he was not turning over the checks. This was excused at first while everyone adjusted to Karen's death and the new situation. Joanne found herself buying all of Christine's clothes, food and diapers, and also paying for medication and some doctor visits. When she asked John for reimbursement for these expenses, he always promised that he would pay her with the next social security check. He paid very little, and soon began to hint at the possibility of having a friend take care of Christine instead of the extended maternal family.

In addition to the expenses, Karen's extended family was also concerned about John's ability to care for Christine. John lived in a very small cabin-like home with wood heat and few amenities. Joanne questioned John's understanding of the needs of a 10-month-old baby. Initially, he did not have a crib for Christine and allowed her to sleep with him. He did not bathe her, and often fed her with the same food that he ate. Christine frequently had diaper rash when he brought her back on Sundays and she had numerous colds and ear infections. Joanne believed that it was not warm enough in John's house, which caused Christine to be ill frequently. Although Joanne felt John was basically a good person and meant well, she was convinced he was not capable of proper parenting for Christine.

Another factor reported by Joanne was that John had very little to do with Christine while Karen was living. Karen confided to Sara shortly before her death that she was planning to leave John. She told her sister they were having problems in their relationship, and that John was more interested in friends and parties than in Karen and Christine. This knowledge fueled the extended family's belief that John was interested in keeping Christine only in order to receive the social security benefits. While the grandparents made it clear they were not interested in taking Christine away from John, they did wish to play an integral part in her life. Sara and Steve were less clear about their intentions.

The first phone conversation with Joanne was un-
usually lengthy because she seemed distraught and des-
perately searching for some solution. Child protection authorities and the attorneys had provided few answers for
her. In fact, she had concluded that litigation, as well as
social services, would only further complicate matters.
During our phone discussion, I explained how mediation
worked, and although she described in great detail her
perception of the problem, I told her I would ask her as
well as others in mediation to disclose everything she had
told me in this phone conversation. I also asked that all
of the people involved with Christine be present at the
initial one-hour consultation. We ended the phone conversation with Joanne agreeing to contact everyone and
attempt to schedule a consultation.

INTAKE PROCEDURE

Joanne called back and set the initial one-hour consultation. She also requested that they schedule a two-hour
mediation session to follow the consultation should they
decide to mediate. Explaining it was difficult to get everyone together, and that John would have to travel 70 miles,
they wanted the opportunity to begin mediation should
they agree to proceed at the end of the consultation. I
told her this was acceptable as I detected an urgency on
the part of Joanne to begin to get this situation settled.

At the initial consultation, everyone seemed tense.
Joanne, Bob, Sara and Steve were all well-dressed. John
came directly from work and had not taken time to clean
up after his job at a fertilizer plant. Sara and Steve sat on
one side of the rectangular table, with Joanne and Bob on
one end, and John sat by himself on the side opposite

Sara and Steve. I positioned myself at the other end facing Joanne and Bob.

I began the consultation by introducing myself and briefly explaining my work. I then asked Joanne to explain why she had initiated this meeting and followed her answer by asking each person at the table to explain why they had chosen to attend. This was actually the first time all had been together to discuss Christine's care. At this point, Sara and Steve, as well as Joanne and Bob, stressed that they were not trying to take Christine away from John, but were only interested in working out better arrangements for her ultimate benefit. By the time John explained his reason for attending, he appeared relieved. He admitted he was afraid they wanted to take Christine away from him, because they thought he was not a good enough father for her. This was an emotional moment which had the effect of relieving the tension, particularly because John seemed sincere in his desire to solve the problem. After this discussion, I spent most of the remaining time speaking about the mediation process, time commitments and costs.

Before any commitment to begin mediation is made, the consultation is used to clarify some of the misperceptions and fears held by the participants. Cutting through the fears is crucial to making progress in the consultation. In this case, as in most, the parties at the table generally act on their best behavior and giving them the opportunity to say why they chose to attend is usually a good opening question. Mediators as well as most therapists understand that only select information is heard by the parties in the first place, and when people are preoccupied with fear, even less information can be assimilated. Therefore, asking clients early in the initial session about their greatest fear is a useful technique. It has the effect of clearing the air as well as having the fears understood and acknowledged by the others in the session. Often, simply talking about the fear will diminish its power and allow the person to participate more fully in the session.

In this case, John was not alone in his fear. Sara, Steve, Joanne and Bob were also intensely fearful that John would cut them out of Christine's life completely. They were also fearful that if they offended John, he could decide to exclude them from Christine's life since he probably had the superior legal position as the natural father of Christine (although the law was never discussed during any of these sessions). Once all had shared their fears, I asked them to reassure each that no one intended to eliminate the other from Christine's life. This allowed them to listen more effectively about my discussion of how I intended to conduct the mediation sessions.

I discussed how the mediation process would work for them by using the facts of their own case. We spoke about Christine and I observed that her interests would not be served by fighting, but rather by improving the cooperation and joint care now being provided by all of them. After answering their questions, I asked if they would sign an Agreement to Begin Mediation adopting our rules about confidentiality of the discussions. All agreed to remain for a two-hour working session.

THE MEDIATION PROCESS

We took a short break and when they returned, I asked each to list the issues they wanted to resolve. No particular order is used during this segment, but each person offers ideas or concerns spontaneously. The comments of one often inspire another's thoughts and concerns and as the issues are raised, I write them on a flip chart, checking to make sure they are recorded correctly.

By giving each person respect, acceptance, and non-judgmental responses, the mediator can create a very positive and comforting emotional setting. At this first stage in the process, it is important not to show either agreement or disagreement with any particular issue. Clients are always looking for the mediator to offer judgments or solutions during the listing of the issues, but the mediator can focus solely on the content without showing bias. Clarification of needs is more important at this point than offering judgmental solutions.

Joanne stated that an important issue for her was the need to eliminate threats from John that he would discontinue the joint care arrangement whenever Joanne asked him for something. I listed on the flip chart, "Christine continue to stay with her grandma and grandpa during the week while her father works" and "Sara provide day care for Christine while Joanne works". She asked that I add "A commitment from John to continue this without threats."

Bob wanted John to be more appreciative of what they were doing for Christine, and to begin paying more of the costs. I wrote, "Work out financial arrangements with John," and asked how I should word the concern about John not appreciating what the family was doing. Bob said it was not necessary to list it, but that he just needed to say it.

Next I turned to Sara, who wanted it clear that she was not trying to take Christine away from John, but that she wanted what was best for Christine. She was very upset about her sister's death, and knew of her sister's plans to leave John before she died. Sara was angry that John was

so possessive about Christine, even though she believed
he had given her little care before Karen's death. Sara
knew that Karen was Christine's primary parent and she
knew Karen was planning to leave John because he was
so immature and didn't like to be tied down with a baby.
Sara now perceived John as hanging onto Christine out
of grief over Karen's death. Sara felt it was in Christine's
best interest to have the consistent care which she could
offer, and to live with Joanne and Bob.

I asked her whether or not she wanted to terminate
John's parental rights to which she replied no. She followed with, "John is her father, and he always will be. I
just wish he could see what was best for her and not be
so possessive of her." I then asked if she would like the
current arrangement to become permanent. She felt it was
best for now or at least until John became more stable in
his employment schedule and his personal life was more
organized. She added that John also needed to learn proper
care for Christine before he could care for her full time.
She was somewhat caught between her belief that she
could provide better care for Christine than John, but still
respecting John for wanting to take care of Christine.

Sara's listing of issues was laden with emotion. I needed
to separate her issues from the emotions. When I began
to record her issues on the flipchart, I began with "Consistent Care for Christine" and clarified whether this was
correct according to her perceptions. Next, I listed
"schedule of care for Christine" and she nodded that this
was another important issue for her. I asked, "Do you
also need to develop a budget of Christine's needs and
a support arrangement to pay for it?" Sara responded that
this would be very helpful, but John would have to agree
to pay for it. I commented that if this was her issue, we

would discuss it and reach agreements, including the financial responsibility for Christine's care.

I then listed, "Parenting Education for John," and asked if this was what she meant when she said that John would have to learn how to take care of Christine. She said she hadn't really thought about how to state it, but it was okay to list it that way. Finally, I asked if she had any other issues, and she added that she was upset about John's feeding of Christine. I asked if they had ever talked with John about this so the diet could be more consistent between the homes. She acknowledged they do not talk very much, so I listed, "better communication among those caring for Christine," and asked if that described her concern about this issue and Sara agreed.

Next, it was John's turn to list issues. He started with wanting Joanne and Sara "to stop bugging him." He complained about Sara and then Joanne "dumping" on him every time he was late or didn't do something just the way they wanted it. Sara and Joanne both began to question what he was saying, but I asked them to hold their thoughts until John was finished with his listing of issues. This was an important intervention because it assured a safe environment for John. Otherwise, he may see himself as being "ganged up on" and becoming the "bad guy" in the discussions.

After this intervention, John relaxed a little for the first time since we began the session. He continued complaining, "They want me to pay for the clothes they buy for Christine, but they are too extravagant. They buy things for Christine that are expensive and impractical because they are cute on her." He felt their choice of clothes was more than he could be expected to pay for out of Christine's Social Security income.

John also expressed the feeling that Karen's family didn't like him and thought that he wasn't good enough to raise Christine. (His response to these fears had been to limit their contact with her and take more control of Christine.) I asked if he felt they had accepted him before Karen's death and he said they all got along quite well. He went on to speak about how he loved Karen very much and how he misses her so much it hurts to talk about it. With tears in his eyes he also acknowledged that he and Karen had not gotten along very well since Christine's birth, and he had some difficulty adjusting to the baby taking so much of Karen's time and attention.

This entire interchange with John was tense and emotional. I waited until he was finished before standing and going to the flip chart to write his issues. I began by softly saying, "John, let me try to write your issues here, and please let me know if I am not writing what you mean." I began by saying, "John, you do not want Joanne and Sara to 'bug' you any more. Could we say that you want a better system of communication with them so you do not feel 'double-teamed' "? He nodded in the affirmative and added that he would like to hear something good about what he does sometimes.

My strategy in the above interaction was to change the issue from a negative perception to a positive goal. John picked up on this immediately with his comment about needing positive feedback as well. I wrote on the flip-chart, "better system of communication" and "positive feedback".

"I also heard you mention their complaint about your being late," I continued. "Do you want to list 'schedules and exchange times' as an issue, or are these clear and working well for all of you?" All answered that these should be listed and several in the room went on to say this was a critical concern. I had apparently uncovered a major issue through turning a complaint into a neutral statement. Listening carefully to what is and what is not said, it is possible to ascertain which are core issues and which are peripheral issues. In this case, the schedule later became the key to reaching acceptable agreement for all, even though some peripheral issues could not be solved in the three sessions held during a six-month period.

Next, I moved to the topic of Christine's expenses and suggested the wording "payment of Christine's expenses." John acknowledged that he should pay, but his question was "for what?" I changed the list of issues to "financial decision-making" and "financial needs determined" and said that they may need to do a budget of Christine's needs and agree on what is reasonable within John's ability to pay before they decide on a method of reimbursement to Sara and Joanne for their expenses. Everyone agreed this was a more accurate statement of the money issue. This intervention narrowed the larger issue of how to pay for Christine's expenses to a more narrow issue of Christine's daily needs and expenses.

I then turned to Steve and asked if he had any issues to be listed. He said no, and he really didn't know if he should be present as he wasn't involved with Christine's care except through hearing Sara's concerns. Everyone kindly encouraged him to continue to be present and he agreed, but declined to offer any other issues.

At this point the flipchart contained the following:

Issues

Christine continue to stay with Joanne during the week

Sara provide day care when Joanne works
John be committed to the above child care of Chris-
   tine
Work out financial arrangements with John
Consistent care for Christine
Schedule of care for Christine
Parenting education for John
Better communication among those caring for Chris-
   tine
Better system of communication
Positive feedback
Schedules and exchange times
Financial decision-making
Financial needs determined
Budget for Christine

I complimented them on completing the list of issues
and commented that many overlapped, indicating they
share many ideas about what was important for Christine. They agreed by acknowledging the similarity of many
issues. I then asked for comments or questions about what
had just been accomplished. Sara said it was hard for her
to listen to what John had to say because she hadn't realized how bad he was feeling or how afraid he was of
the family taking Christine from him. Sara spoke of her
fear that John wanted to take Christine from the rest of
the family. John said he felt better knowing that everyone
was so interested in helping rather than in simply trying
to remove Christine. Joanne added that it was hard enough
losing Karen, she did not want to also lose Christine or
John: "After all, maybe we really need each other more
than we know, and we all need Christine, too. Karen's
death was hard for each of us and we know that now."

I felt tears in my own eyes as they talked briefly about Karen and their need to talk like this more often. So far, the discussions had cleared away many of their misperceptions. Moreover, some much needed common grieving about Karen's death had surfaced. They each appeared hurt and angry about her death and seemed to have dealt with it only individually and privately. While this was not a mediation issue, it certainly was an important aspect of their present conflict concerning Christine's care. In the session I encouraged them to talk about their emotional pain and discuss it to the extent that they were comfortable. My strategy was to keep this from becoming a potential roadblock or impasse. Had they not discussed it then, it would have certainly surfaced later and might have become detrimental to the settlement process.

We took a five-minute break and, when we returned, categorized the list of issues into four main topic areas: care of Christine; finances and expenses; parenting education for John; and communication about Christine. I directed them to first discuss the arrangements for Christine's care because the schedule of exchanges seemed to be the easiest issue on which to obtain consensus.

Care of Christine

I went to the flip chart and drew a four-week parenting schedule grid and then asked them to give me the present parenting schedule. Christine lives with John who is her primary caretaker. However, he works Monday through Friday from 7:30 a.m. to 4:30 p.m. at the fertilizer plant. On Sundays he brings Christine to Joanne's to stay for the week while he works, and picks her up again on Fridays after work or on Saturdays. Sometimes he stays at Joanne and Bob's house for the weekend rather than taking Christine back to his home. About every third weekend Christine stays all weekend with her grandparents, and then John usually comes to see her one or two evenings during the week.

This schedule was never written or discussed with any particular planning. Instead, it had become fairly spontaneous, and it was up to John as to when the time of exchanges actually took place. This worked for a time, but became less desirable after a few weeks when Joanne began to feel used. Joanne found herself unable to plan her weekends or even weekday evenings without a long-distance phone call to John. To complicate matters, John did not always follow through on his commitments about time even when planned in advance.

Since they did not have a regular schedule, I asked what they each felt was important in a future schedule. This helped to remove past problems from the discussions and focused on what would work better in the future. They all agreed it was in Christine's best interests to be cared for by her grandmother and aunt if they could agree on the schedule and procedures. Next, they agreed that Christine would spend weekdays and nights with Joanne and Bob, and Sara would provide day care. I filled the grid of squares by placing a "G" for grandparents in the Monday through Friday square. Next, I asked about the weekends. John said he wanted Christine at home every weekend except when he was on call for work, which occurred about every fourth week. I filled in Saturday and Sunday of weeks one through three with "D" for Dad and asked Joanne if she was comfortable with that. She said she would like to have Christine at least one weekend in four, because during the weekdays, she only saw her in the morning and at night and seldom had additional time with her "just for fun and routines." They agreed that the fourth weekend Saturday and Sunday would be filled with "G." Sara interjected that she too would like an overnight with Christine at her home. Joanne agreed that this would be easiest for her on Wednesday evenings when she had choir practice. Now the schedule had an "A" for aunt on Wednesday nights. John said that was fine with him, except he would like Christine with him on the Wednesday night preceding his on-call weekend. They all agreed that this was fair and the least complicated for everyone.

My next goal was to focus on the narrow issue of the exact time of the exchanges. This had irritated Joanne and Bob in the past, because John never seemed to arrive on time to pick up Christine even though he would promise to arrive at a certain time. I turned to John and asked him what time he could consistently commit to picking up Christine on Fridays or Saturdays. He struggled about this because weekends were the only time he could socialize "with the guys," yet this was the only time he had to be with Christine. He asked if he could pick her up at 8:30 p.m. Fridays so he could have some time to go out after work on Fridays. Joanne did not like this, saying, "Christine goes to bed at 8:00 p.m. and it isn't good to be traveling with her so late." She also voiced her worry about his drinking with the guys and then driving with Christine. This was obviously a sensitive issue. Even Bob entered this one with his own criticism of John needing to choose between his own pleasure and being a parent to Christine.

I again posed a question to John, "Do you understand their concerns about this?" He understood, yet he expressed concern about their acting like his parents rather than Christine's grandparents. He felt they wanted to control his life, requiring him to act according to their rules. He suggested, "Maybe it would be best for Christine to stay with me all of the time and go to a day care home near me. You could come and visit her whenever you want on weekends if I don't have plans." At this point, the tension in the room rose above the boiling point.

I calmly retraced where we had come in the discussions. "You are agreed it would be in Christine's best interests for her to live with her father, stay with her grandparents during the week, and have day care provided by her aunt, right?" I said. They all nodded in the affirmative. "Why?" I asked. "Because we are the people closest to her," Joanne answered. "We care more about her than anyone else," Sara added. John said, "She just lost her mother, and she needs all of us to take care of her and love her. It's the best thing next to her mother." Each also expressed a need to have time away from Christine, with their own partners and friends. "But you all have your own personal lives too, isn't that right? So how can you make this schedule work for all of you and for Christine?" I asked. John looked at the schedule on the flip chart and asked if it would be okay if he picked Christine up on the first and third Fridays at 6:00 p.m.— he'd come right from work. Then on the second week he would come on Saturday mornings at 9:00 a.m. Joanne said that would be fine, and he could have dinner with them on the Friday evenings, giving her an opportunity to explain to him about Christine's week. Bob apologized for his earlier comment and agreed that this would be fine with him. He acknowledged that John needed time with friends, just like everyone else. Sara liked this solu-

	Mon	Tue	Wed	Thu	Fri	Sat	Sun
	G = Grandparents			A = Aunt		D = Dad	
Week 1	G	G	G/A	A/G	G/D	D	D/G
Week 2	G	G	G/A	A/G	G	G/D	D/G
Week 3	G	G	G/A	A/G	G/D	D	D/G
Week 4	G	G	G/D	D/G	G	G	G

tion and was relieved that the whole discussion did not go up in smoke. I filled in the entire schedule with the exchange times as indicated above.

This includes day care with Aunt Sara every day, Monday through Friday.

Finances and Expenses

The next issue on my agenda concerned the financial arrangements. John said that he receives $220.00 per month for Christine from Social Security Survivors Benefits, and he nets approximately $650.00 per month from his employment. His house payment is $280.00 per month, and utilities and groceries cost him another $300.00 per month. He also has to buy gas, clothes, etc. He said he is broke all of the time. He offered to pay Joanne and Sara the entire social security money, but said he could not afford to pay any more than that. He still intended to buy some clothes for Christine and would provide diapers for her during the week. Joanne questioned how he could afford all of that, and he said he can earn extra money through overtime if he puts his name in early.

Joanne and Sara agreed that the Social Security check would be sufficient, and if their expenses were higher, they would contribute it to Christine and not complain to John about it. Everyone in the room agreed that the costs of raising Christine were much greater than what the Social Security check provided, but they each were committed to making sure that she had everything she needed.

Parenting Education

This issue was raised by Sara because she was so concerned about John's lack of knowledge to take care of Christine's basic needs. She complained about John taking Christine out for pizza which made her ill for three days, and also about her bedtime. Joanne also asked what John does with her on weekends, because she is never at home even late at night. John said he did not like leaving her with babysitters, so he always took her with him. He admitted that he didn't know about her diet and thought she was old enough to eat table food. He was not doing that any longer after Joanne explained to him what Christine's diet should be. Sara also felt that John plays too roughly with Christine; an example was that he tosses her about a foot above his head and catches her. Sara suggested that this was a dangerous practice, and that what she really needed was a lot of touching, eye contact and talking to her. John said he just never had a baby before and was doing what he thought was right.

I intervened at this point. John had heard a lot of negative criticism and was becoming defensive. I empathized with John about not knowing how to take care of a baby and asked him if he would be interested in attending a class which teaches fathers of babies how to take care of them. This took the pressure off John and normalized the situation for him. He responded with an interest in joining such a class. I asked the others in the room if they felt this might be a way of beginning to resolve this concern. They all agreed it would. John agreed to enroll as soon as possible.

Communication About Christine

The fourth category of issues was communication. There were numerous indications in the discussions that John and the others did not successfully communicate very much about Christine. I began by asking how they exchanged information now about Christine. They apparently talked briefly at the times of the exchanges and sometimes wrote some things down. But most of the communication was in the form of complaints.

Since time was running short in the session, I suggested some rules about communication:

1. Spend at least 10 minutes at each exchange time sitting down at a table to talk about Christine.
2. Express complaints as concerns and offer positive alternatives to the complaints.
3. Keep a notebook of important information about Christine, developmental changes, medical needs, changes in routine or diet, etc.
5. Phone each other about any changes in schedules at least 24 hours in advance, and notify each other if someone has to be late at exchange times.

6. If anyone is unsure about a message or anything, call the other person involved.
7. Always be open and honest with each other, and place Christine's interests first.
8. Trust each other that you are each doing your best.

They agreed that they would follow these rules and add to them as needed. They reviewed all of the progress that they had made in these two hours and agreed that they may not have to meet again. I did suggest that they try out their decisions for a period of approximately four months and review and make changes then. I also asked them to let me know how things were going.

SECOND SESSION

About four months after our last session, Joanne called to schedule another session. This time she was very upset because John had decided to put Christine in day care with a friend in his town. I called John and asked him if he would come to another session. He reluctantly agreed though he was angry at Joanne and Sara about something.

When we met, we first reviewed the decisions reached four months earlier. John was quite defensive and angry. Joanne was also quite upset. About a month ago John announced that a friend of his had offered to take care of Christine while he worked. She had a day care business in her home, and there were two other children about Christine's age there. Without making any judgment, I changed the subject back to their earlier decisions.

They had begun to operate on a much better level after the last session. In fact, John and Bob had even spent some time together fishing and getting to know each other better. Christine was doing very well. Then about six weeks ago Bob and Joanne stopped in to pick up some fishing gear at John's on a weekend when Christine was with him. As they walked up to the house they heard Christine crying. They knocked on the door but no one answered. It was unlocked so they went in and found Christine alone in her play pen with the dog barking to keep them away from her. She was dirty and wet, and there was dried food on plates on the table and empty beer cans strewn about.

Needless to say, Joanne was very upset. She had not been in John's house since Karen died so the condition was appalling to her. Karen had always kept it neat and clean. Bob coaxed the dog outside and went to look for John while Joanne took care of Christine who was so happy to see her. John was over at the neighbor's chopping wood while Christine was napping. He was very embarrassed about the condition of the house but felt it was okay to leave Christine napping with the dog there while he chopped wood. This incident did not rest well with Joanne, and she began to question John's care of Christine each time he brought her and picked her up at Joanne's house.

Well, the process had once again slipped back into the incident at John's house. Again I carefully avoided any judgment and returned to the agreement of four months earlier. In reviewing it Joanne asked John what classes he had attended about parenting Christine. John defensively retorted that he hadn't had any time to look into it. He went on to say that the day Joanne and Bob stopped in was just the worst time. He said he usually kept the house quite clean, but that it was the third anniversary of when he and Karen met, and he had been very down. Some friends tried to cheer him up by bringing some beer over, but he drank too much and fell asleep. He added that he thought it would be more like a family if Christine stayed with him all of the time, and maybe then he'd get better about staying home and keeping house rather than going out with his friends all of the time. "After all," he said, "she is my daughter and I'm her father."

Joanne was visibly upset and her eyes welled up with tears. After all her worst fears had been realized—John was going to keep Christine from them. I quietly intervened with the question, "John, what do you really think is best for Christine?" He replied, "I don't know, I don't know, maybe I should just disappear." When I was a child protection worker I used to call this state of affairs "rock bottom," and I think this was not very different. I asked John another question, "Doesn't Christine need her dad as much as she needs everyone in this room?" He said quietly, "Yes."

I took control of the session with, "You are all here today because you love a little girl who has lost her mom and now you are each the most important people in her life. What agreements can you make to get back on track so you can each give her the love you have for her?" Joanne turned to John and asked him if he would reconsider and continue to allow her to have Christine during the week while he worked. She even suggested that perhaps Bob or she could drive Christine one way each weekend so there wouldn't be so much of a burden on John. Sara also asked for this and added that Christine had just joined a play group of other children her age and she just loved it. John said it was just so hard being away from her all week, but that it was probably best for her.

By the end of the two hours, they agreed to give their former arrangements another chance. John said he did check into a parenting class, but it met on Saturday mornings for eight weeks and it just didn't fit with his schedule, so he was checking on another that meets Wednesday evenings, and he would go to that. They also agreed that they would call me and meet within two months to review all of this.

THIRD SESSION

Two months later Joanne called and scheduled another session. She indicated that there were still problems and she was not at all optimistic. She also said that John wanted his father present at the next session.

This time we met with everyone, plus John's father, Joe. Once again Joanne opened the session with a concern about John playing so much baseball that he has little time for Christine even when she is with him. Christine was now 16 months old, walking and trying to talk. Everyone was enjoying her and no one complained that she was having any difficulties.

I began the session by reviewing the first and second sessions and then asked what had transpired since our last session. John said he had joined his baseball team again. This had been a special event when Karen was living—they always went to the ball games and out to a "kegger" afterwards with friends before going home. Joanne complained that John took Christine to the games and let her run around unsupervised while he played, then took her to the parties and she was becoming very exhausted and having more ear infections and colds than usual. John did not go to the parenting classes because of the baseball schedule and promised that he would go next fall. Sara also was angry at John because she felt that she had to always care for a sick baby because John did not see that she got her sleep and medications.

This discussion continued and I directed it towards what they wanted to do to change the present course of events. Joanne was very pessimistic. She reiterated to John that she was not trying to take Christine away from John; in fact she wished John would change his ways so that he could be a better, more responsible father for her. Bob agreed saying he understood John's interest in playing ball, but that it didn't fit with the responsibilities of a single father. Bob felt that Christine needed more than John could give her right now. Steve, who usually said nothing at these sessions, also agreed that Christine was such a wonderful child he just couldn't understand why John wouldn't give up some of his pleasures for her sake. Of course, Steve was five years older, married and professionally employed so his whole lifestyle was very different than John's.

I tried to summarize where we were in this session when Joe asked if he could say something. I welcomed his request. Joe said he had been listening to everything everyone had been saying, and that what he was about to say may be hard to hear, but he felt he had to say it. He turned to John, "I know you have been through a lot this past year with Karen's death and all. And I respect you for what you are trying to do with Christine. But I don't think you realize what you have here. Here are Christine's grandparents, her aunt and uncle and even me and your stepmom all willing to do everything we can to help you raise Christine. You are still a young fellow and it's got to be hard being tied down with a baby when you should be having fun with friends and building a future for yourself. It seems to me that you could do a lot better than you are right now. If you really want to keep Christine—and I don't hear anyone here trying to take her away from you—maybe you have to quit that job of yours, move into town nearer to all of us, get a decent apartment and a regular job. Then we can all help you raise her. But you have to decide what you're going to do. Why can't you try that? Your stepmom and I have been trying to get you to move into town since Karen died, and now I understand that these people would also like to be closer to you and Christine. What do you think?"

John had listened intently and questioned whether or not he could find employment. His dad said he'd help him, and so did Bob and Steve. Joanne was very relieved to hear Joe's comments and asked John if he'd do that for Christine. He said he would.

CONCLUSION

A mediator never predicts outcomes, but I usually have an idea as to how things will finally work out. In this case, however, I was totally surprised. I thought that Joe's joining the session meant that John would have a stronger advocate and that settlement would be remote. This turn in events was what was needed to turn things around for everyone.

As I analyze this, I note that the most important strategy throughout this mediation was not to agree with anyone but to acknowledge the importance of each person's perspective and to keep the discussions on a constructive level. This case, more than most, presented some challenges to my mediation skills because I continually found myself questioning whether or not the child was being harmed. I did not impose my values and I discouraged others from doing so, but allowed them to raise concerns only about the care and parenting of Christine and offer their ideas about what would be best for her. For me, focusing on Christine kept me from being pulled into the middle of this and issuing advice and opinions. As it turned out, the parties to the problem resolved it themselves and can go on respecting each other because they worked so hard to care for Christine.

7

Perceptions of Power in Mediation: Case Examples of Power Imbalance

A recurring objection voiced mainly by some litigious divorce attorneys about mediation has been the so called "power imbalance," or the lack of power of the "weaker party," a euphemism for "wife." It is only logical that legal advocates would be critical of a system that relies on the parties themselves to settle issues without outside assistance from those professional advocates. However, to criticize mediation solely on the ground that the weaker party always gives away the farm in order to obtain a peaceful settlement fails to take into account that a con-

vincing case has already been made that wives tend to
fare poorly in the court process (Weitzman, 1985).

Power, for purposes of our discussion, is simply the
differences in the strengths and weaknesses of the parties. While many observers of negotiations attempt to
measure who has more or less power, we are more concerned with how a mediator manages the inappropriate
use of power. Seldom is it the case that one person holds
all the cards. Usually, both husband and wife become very
adept at destructive methods of using power. Only a beginning log of the various categories of inappropriate
power usage is attempted. Indeed, in our culture, a whole
new treatment specialty has emerged in the past decade
which focuses on codependency and attempts to assist
people in finding the power to break free of destructive
relationships.

How these differences affect the mediator's role should
necessarily be part of every mediator's concern because
the couple's perceptions about power often become roadblocks (primarily in their own eyes) to settlement. However, we suggest that fear about power imbalances need
not become a reason for concluding that some couples
are inappropriate for mediation provided certain strategies and techniques are used to minimize the destructive
impact of the inappropriate use of power. Divorce is usually based upon "irreconcilable differences," and therefore the parties' differences are central to every divorce
mediation. The task for the mediator lies in learning these
differences and how they influence the process of making
decisions about the settlement. In this chapter, we have
chosen several case examples to illustrate how power differences can influence the mediation process and how the
mediator might deal with these seemingly irreconcilable

differences as well as with each couple's tendency to employ one or more destructive uses of power.

The inappropriate use of power takes many forms. In the legal system it might be the large law firm deciding to keep its smaller opponent knee deep in interrogatories, hoping to bury the other side in procedural costs and delays. In the mediation room, it might be the husband's threat to initiate a costly and damaging custody battle in order to obtain a more favorable property or spousal support settlement. In the intact marriage, it might be the withholding of sexual activities by either spouse to make a point or score a victory in an argument about something unrelated to the bedroom. In almost every case of misuse of power, the real issue is buried somewhere else. The important point stressed in the following cases is that patience, perseverance and a large dose of kindness on the part of the mediator often tend to smoke out the real issue. Once the core concerns are exposed, they can then be discussed and resolved. The important concept for the mediator to remember is not who has the most power (because it is really incapable of being measured), but what concern lies beneath each attempt to gain power.

HOMEMAKER WIFE AND CAREER TEACHER HUSBAND— MEREDITH AND PERRY

Perry and Meredith came to mediation while they still lived together and neither had consulted with an attorney about a divorce. Perry had been in therapy for the last nine years working on his own feelings of insecurity and low self-esteem as a result of being raised in an alcoholic family system. Meredith had not been in therapy and was threatened by Perry's positive personality changes. "Look at him, he's got it all together, he knows what he wants and he's going to do just fine; Mr. Perfect," she would say about him. Perry is a teacher, likes his job, is tenured, and earns approximately $40,000.00 per year. He is tall, thin and attractive. Meredith is self-employed in the home as a piano teacher and earns about $6,000.00 per year. She is depressed, overweight, and angry.

During their 19-year marriage, they could never agree on spending money, and had opposite philosophies about necessary and discretionary spending. Each handled his or her own money from earnings, and Perry paid for most of the family bills, other than charge accounts, which he did not believe in. Meredith purchased clothing and other household items for herself and the children. She sometimes charged these items when she did not have enough cash. Perry bought most of the groceries, but Meredith bought snacks and was soundly criticized for this by Perry. In mediation, their conflict centered around money, though they were extremely hostile toward each other about parenting and most other areas as well.

Until Perry entered therapy, they described their marriage as less conflicted—each just went along with the way things happened. Meredith was more satisfied with that and never understood Perry's decision to enter therapy. He wanted her to be involved in therapy and she resisted the message she heard that there might be something wrong with her.

Perry and Meredith have two children, Stephanie, age 12, and Michael, age 16. Both admitted their reason for not separating earlier was concern for the children. Neither wanted to leave the children nor the house (which was fully paid for). The children frequently overheard threats of divorce, though they never took them seriously since neither parent had taken any steps toward a divorce. Michael was looking toward his future independence from the family, and his friends were more important to him than his family at this point in his life. Stephanie was very close to each of her parents and reacted with crying when they had especially rageful fights. She was no doubt affected by the family's dysfunction, yet she did not want her parents to get a divorce.

When Meredith and Perry attended the consultation session to discuss divorce mediation, it was the first step either had taken toward a divorce, and it was initiated by Perry. The first impression was that Perry was the strong dominant party, and that Meredith appeared extremely weak, depressed, and unknowledgeable. The consultation was difficult. Perry began by answering most of the mediator's questions, describing his perception of the marital problems and their need to go ahead with the divorce. Meredith just sat and listened, commenting that he wanted the divorce and she was just going to be quiet.

If we stop and analyze what we know about this case at this point, most critics of mediation would say that this couple is not appropriate for mediation because of the obvious "power imbalance" between Perry and Meredith. They would insist that the mediator refer them to lawyers so that Meredith could have a lawyer speak for her and take care of her needs by getting information from Perry through interrogatories and depositions so that Meredith never had to speak to him. Her lawyer would probably schedule a temporary hearing and ask the court to order Perry out of the house, granting temporary custody to Meredith and allowing Perry every other weekend and Wednesday night visitations, have him pay her 30% (in Minnesota) of his net income as child support, and set reasonable alimony.

The mediator proceeded with the consultation by asking whether they have discussed any plans for the parenting of the children. Perry said, "We have not even been able to talk about what to have for supper, much less the parenting of the children." He paused and then added, "I would like to have a major role in the parenting of the children after the divorce." Meredith reacted sarcastically with, "What kind of a parent do you think you could be—you wouldn't even buy clothes for them!" And then she began to scream and wail. She was hurt and angry, and had listened as long as she could without responding. She attacked him again for looking so "together," and cried loudly about her needs and the fact that she had raised the children to this point without much assistance from him, and with no financial help from him for all the children's extracurricular activities. She said she takes on extra piano students to pay for the children's lessons and athletic training and equipment. She also said that she wanted Perry out of the house so she could restore some order to the children's lives as well as to her own. She regained her composure a bit and went on to say that she does not intend to take the children away from him, because the children love him, but that she is not going to sit and agree with him just because he looks so "together."

Arguably, the perception of power has changed. Some observers might say that Perry may now get the short end of the stick because Meredith has more power in the mediation room through her emotional displays and her ability to put down her husband as the uncaring, distant father.

Neither of these perceptions of power is accurate. The power in the room actually floats from one to the other throughout the mediation process. These fluctuations in apparent power were evident throughout the remaining six mediation sessions, making it a very difficult mediation for the mediator to conduct. At times they both yelled at each other as loudly as they could, and the mediator had to insist that they be quiet or end the session. At other times they talked very caringly about each other and their children.

Meredith and Perry finally settled on an agreement that had Perry move out of the house into an apartment near the school. The children attended a mediation session near the end, and were asked by their parents to try an exchange schedule for a trial period of three months. At that session, all of the property and financial issues had been settled, and the children were asked what they thought of a schedule that had them moving from each parent's house every two weeks. Michael, the husky athlete, replied, "I don't care what the two of you do, I just want to stay in the house in my own room," a predictable response for a 16-year-old. When Stephanie was asked the same question, she tearfully responded, "I just want to be where my big brother is." Michael, now also tearful, said, "I suppose we can try it." After the six-week trial period, the entire family agreed that the schedule would work for each of them.

The case settled with Perry receiving one-third of the property, including all of the marital debt, and with Meredith receiving two-thirds of the marital property, including the home which had no mortgage and no marital debt. The parenting arrangement was shared, with each having the children one-half of the time, and Perry paying child support for the children's needs while they were with Meredith. They agreed that the unequal division of the property was in lieu of spousal support, and that Meredith will have enough income from her teaching to meet her needs adequately because there was no house payment. Both were very satisfied with the settlement, which they said met both of their needs at the time.

Perry continued to have greater control over his emotions than Meredith. Through her outbursts she showed symptoms of not understanding or being overwhelmed. The mediator handled the outbursts respectfully, always calming her down, then probing for the cause and, upon learning it, directing the search for a solution so that she could again regain composure and go on. The mediator asked her to talk to her therapist about the emotions so she could begin to minimize the need for the outbursts. Meredith agreed, in hopes of alleviating some of the pain of the divorce she did not want. She also investigated the possibility of returning to school to enhance her employability. Both Perry and Meredith continued to express their feelings angrily and loudly, although they apologized for it and controlled the length of the outbursts, often referring to the cost of mediation as a motivator. Perry shared all financial information openly, as did Meredith, by bringing in all documentation of assets when requested by the mediator.

Despite Perry's healthy-looking demeanor, he was very sad and angry about the divorce. He felt guilty about pushing it forward, though he was convinced of its necessity for his own mental health as well as for the emotional well-being of the children. He also hoped it would be healthy for Meredith, and was especially pleased about her beginning therapy. Although Perry seemed to have an excess of power at the onset of mediation, this was minimized during the process by his sharing with Meredith his knowledge about finances and frugal living, as well as through his willingness to pay adequate child support in addition to the unequal division of marital property. At the end of mediation, his main regret was that he had not moved to get the divorce earlier, before Meredith had used so much credit and thereby created debt which depleted the value of the total marital assets.

Mediator Strategies

The following are some of the strategies used to dissipate any perceived or real power imbalances:

1. **Promoting reality:** From the very beginning, we talked about the divorce although Meredith was opposed to it. I also dealt with the reality of Meredith's feelings and assisted her in seeking therapy. This also had the effect of normalizing her behavior in the sessions. She was told it is normal to feel angry, hurt, rejected, etc., when going through a divorce. The question was how to manage those feelings so they would not adversely affect the mediation process. This empowered her to make some choices about how she could get her needs met in mediation. She began to accept the fact that she was in the midst of her own divorce, and with that acceptance, she was then better able to function in her decision-making in mediation.

2. **Informal rules:** I laid down the rule about not allowing cheap shots at the very beginning. However, until
   they began to control their emotions, I intervened frequently to halt the cheap shots. This began to assure
   a safe environment, and didn't allow the blame and
   faultfinding to influence their decision-making. To some
   extent this also neutralized their perceptions of the
   other's power. I took away the weapons that kept them
   competitive and operating from their perceptions of
   power. By being asked to make "I" statements, they
   began to take charge of the issues and their own needs
   and to cooperate.

3. **Bargaining from interests:** They each took the position
   that the other was not a good parent. Perry was convinced that Meredith's emotional neediness was detrimental to the children and that she parented out of
   her own needs rather than those of the children. I addressed that issue by asking what he wanted as a parenting arrangement, to which he immediately replied
   that he didn't want to take the children away from
   Meredith. I asked again, "What do you want in a parenting arrangement for your children?" He finally began to understand that degrading her did not give him
   any advantage or power in deciding the parenting arrangements, because in mediation he was asked to state
   exactly what he wanted in order to fulfill his own future needs as a parent.

4. **Defining the issues:** When I defined the financial issues in terms of separate responsibilities, they were
   less able to control the other. Perry first said he would
   support the children in Meredith's home by buying
   specific items for them rather than paying child support to Meredith and allowing her to be responsible
   for providing for the children's needs while they lived

with her. I intervened by asking them to make a budget of the children's needs before deciding who would be responsible for what items. Perry made sure that they both understood exactly what each of their financial responsibilities concerning budget items for the children were, and I recorded their entire budget on the flip chart as well as in their final agreement. Perry was then able to agree to pay Meredith direct child support, and Meredith was more comfortable knowing that Perry would not interfere with her spending decisions.

SUCCESSFUL BUSINESSMAN AND PARTNER/WIFE—
TOM AND CAROL

Carol telephoned the mediation office and insisted on speaking directly with a mediator. She was very distraught. She and Tom were in the midst of a court battle and he was dragging his feet because he did not want the divorce. She said that he didn't care if all of the assets were eaten up in the divorce battle. They had already spent $18,000.00 in combined attorneys' fees and had accomplished only a temporary hearing after 10 months of litigation. She asked if a mediator would call her husband to see if he would come with her to an initial consultation. We first sent out packets of information to each of them with a cover letter explaining Carol's request. This was followed by a phone call to Tom a few days later. Tom was very willing to attend a consultation session and scheduled one immediately.

The initial consultation lasted about one hour, with Carol dominating the discussion. She accused Tom of unfaithfulness and disclosed that he suffers from a manic/depressive mental disorder. Because of this disorder, she insisted that he was incapable of managing money and the business, and suggested that they transfer the business decision-making to one of their sons. She also demanded the homestead and half of the business assets. Tom agreed with everything that she said and acted very lovingly toward her. Tom was very quiet, nodding his agreement to everything she said and seemed very amenable and kind. Carol then raised the issue of Tom's religious beliefs—that he has joined a cult type of group that was not Christian, and preached the simple life, health foods and holistic medicine. Tom acknowledged this by saying how fortunate it was for Carol because she could have everything—and he would be fine with very little in material assets. Tom was so passive in this consultation, and Carol so aggressive, that if the divorce were settled right then, Tom would have signed off on everything and Carol would have been very happy.

At the consultation, it seemed that Carol could overpower Tom easily through her use of guilt and charm. I explained thoroughly my role as a mediator and emphasized that a mutual standard of fairness was necessary for a lasting, workable agreement. I also emphasized the need to have full and complete disclosure of all information and facts before final decisions were made. I said that although their settlement ideas expressed at the consultation could later become adopted decisions, I insisted upon following the steps in the mediation process so as to ensure that the settlement would hold up in the eyes of their attorneys. They both agreed, and began mediation.

The first session had a turbulent beginning. Tom was depressed and angry. His mood was resentful of Carol, and he attacked her with verbal tirades about her insistence on the divorce and the belief that she was "turning the children against him." My impressions from the initial consultation were dashed. This couple was highly conflicted and verbally abusive to each other in session. Tom was no longer as passive as he was in the consultation, and Carol seemed mild and "weak" in comparison to Tom. They were not cooperative. Although Tom appeared powerful with his booming, angry voice, Carol could regain control by simply letting Tom rage on. When she did reply, it was very cutting and very skillfully designed to put Tom down. I immediately took control by directing them both to the flip chart.

The dispute was mainly over the marital assets. Carol lived in the house, and Tom operated the business which employed Carol. Tom no longer took her on buying trips and did not send her to sales promotion meetings. One of their sons, however, was closely associated with the business and Carol learned all she wanted from him. Tom was accustomed to controlling all of the money, and providing Carol with whatever she needed. He enjoyed that role, and now was upset about the court order that required him to pay support as well as allowing her to take over management of the house. He wanted her signature on another business loan, and she enjoyed the power she experienced by refusing to sign. She almost seemed to enjoy Tom's frustrations.

Both Tom and Carol were experts at the games, but both had become weary of the battle. Each perceived the other as very powerful and herself or himself as weak. Carol was well-dressed, intelligent, and very close to the children. Tom was a master at the business and had made it very profitable after buying it from his father and siblings, but he had difficulties in personal relationships and was not tolerant of the children. In reality, both had significant power, but both were misusing their power.

After four two-hour mediation sessions, Tom and Carol arrived at a settlement both felt was fair. The two minor children lived primarily with Carol, and Tom paid generous child support well in excess of the state child support guidelines which would have been grossly insufficient considering their lifestyles. Carol kept the house and Tom kept the business. To offset the difference in the values, Carol was given income property which provided her with a substantial monthly income. Both waived spousal support in order to eliminate the connectedness of monthly support exchanges. Each said they were pleased with the outcome, and their attorneys raised no objections to the settlement, even though it was not a typical settlement that might be predicted from court litigation.

Mediator Strategies

The following are some of the strategies I used to mediate this case of competing powers.

1. **Respect:** This case was particularly difficult because they attempted to transfer the tension and stress of the divorce by projecting anger toward the mediator. Each seemed to use anger as a method of attaining power. Their anger began to melt each time an angry outburst was met with "Unconditional Positive Regard" (Rogers, 1951). That is, when the concern expressed in each angry outburst was validated and respected, both soon

began to interact using less angry communication patterns.

2. **Emotional control:** Coupled with respect, another mediation strategy used was a soft voice. Mediators are very successful in handling loudness and yelling by leaning forward, making eye contact and speaking softly. This has a calming effect, and also forces them to be quiet in order to hear what is being said. When Tom yelled, I waited and then leaned over to him and asked if he could express his thoughts in a less stressful way. I often interrupted loudness with a quiet question of clarification which usually brought the person out of anger and back to the issue at hand.

3. **Create understanding:** Taking anger seriously is a very effective strategy. Anger in a relationship is often tuned out by one party. In mediation, anger must be taken seriously. The rule imposed here is: Anything that is said must be understood by all in the room. Therefore, I ask what is meant by an angry statement. Soon the parties both learn that spurious statements will come under scrutiny and they will avoid them as not being in either of their interests. In a sense, the requirement that both must understand each statement made in the room requires each to process and integrate the information. Through this process, the attempts by each to control and frustrate the other give way to a mediator's request that problems be continually attacked, instead of each party being attacked.

4. **Informal rules:** Enforcing the rule, "Speak only for yourself in the first person" usually kept their button-pushing to a minimum. At first, this particular rule needed to be continually restated, but as it became assimilated by them, Tom and Carol often stopped

themselves in the middle of a statement and referred to it as they reframed their thought. When Carol accused Tom of being harsh with the children, I asked her what she would like Tom to do that would work better in his relationship with the children. The rule imposed here was, "A negative criticism must be followed by a positive alternative." Carol followed with, "I would like Tom to spend more time with the children doing the children's agenda and not his own."

Tom listened to her and told her he appreciated that suggestion and would try it. She continued by giving him some ideas about what the children may enjoy doing with him. She also promised to encourage the children to spend time with Tom.

The key to mediating the power differences in this case was the mediator's efforts in demonstrating that their angry power plays did not meet their needs, while open, honest communication did.

As is so often the case, couples such as Tom and Carol are successful in most other areas of their lives, be it business or parenting. Because their system of relating to each other becomes dysfunctional, it appears that one is more powerful or less powerful. Through rigorous management of what amounts to almost infantile behavior, the cycle of destructive behavior can be changed and acceptable agreements reached.

HOW DO I KNOW THAT HE'S NOT HIDING SOMETHING?— MARK AND JEAN

The most often asked question by women considering divorce mediation is: "How do I know he's not hiding something?" and the most common answer is, "You don't, but there are many ways to find out." Although concealment of assets is often used as a reason given by attorneys to discourage women from entering mediation, it is rare in divorce mediation as well as in the adversarial system. The message given by some attorneys is that the mediation process will not protect wives from husbands hiding marital assets and therefore "you should not consider doing something that will ultimately harm you." The truth is that both systems have measures for ensuring that assets and income are disclosed. These measures are tax returns, examination of bank records, verification of values through appraisals, documents and many other measures to arrive at factual truth. In both systems, the skill of the professional employed by the parties operates to ensure that full disclosure occurs. Sometimes, out of fear or greed or simple dishonesty, the requirement of honest full disclosure is thwarted through a person's attempt to garner power, as in the case of Mark and Jean.

It was a typical divorce where the husband was seeing another woman and the wife discovered his affair and promptly filed for divorce. They had seen a therapist to attempt reconciliation, but that was not successful.

Mark and Jean were both in their mid-fifties. Mark operated his own business out of the family home, and Jean was a homemaker. Two of their three children were grown and the youngest, Robby, was in junior high. The divorce petition ordered Mark to leave the home, which he obediently did, thinking the whole thing would blow over. When Jean did not relent, he called the mediation office for information. He shared it with Jean and they both came for the initial consultation. Mark was a good businessman and earned a comfortable income for the family.

Jean had never worked outside the home. Mark handled all of the finances and made all of the financial decisions and Jean ran the home. Jean was totally in the dark when we reviewed the questionnaire each was required to complete in preparation for the first session. She did have the information for the budgets, but didn't know anything about their assets and liabilities. Mark was just the opposite, aware of their net worth, but with little knowledge of what they spent each month. We talked about how mediation would be a learning experience for both of them. After discussion and questions, they decided to proceed with the mediation process.

The first session went smoothly with the gathering of information about the assets and liabilities. Jean felt at a disadvantage so she was given homework to obtain information about various assets and liabilities. Mark was asked to get an appraisal of the business and Jean was in charge of the appraisal of the house. They both were to meet with the appraisers and were present during all discussions about the house and business assets. Their homework items were established and at the next session they would begin the discussion about values.

Next they discussed their minor child, Robby. Jean insisted that Robby remain in the home with her so that his life would be disrupted as little as possible. Mark quietly agreed, though he wasn't convinced that was best. They discussed other parenting agreements about Robby and then they moved to the topic of spousal support. Jean became very defensive when Mark asked her if she was going to work. It soon became apparent that the family income would not be sufficient to cover the costs of two households.

The issues were all before them like pieces of a puzzle to be put in place, each one contingent to some extent on the others. Both Jean and Mark were overwhelmed with the extent of choices they had to make.

If we stop here and analyze the power issues, this looks like the classic powerful husband and weak wife. Yet the power shifted when they were asked to obtain the appraisals. Each was given a task, yet they were both expected to cooperate in the meetings with the appraisers. There was a sharing of the power through the expectation that they both meet with the appraisers and learn about the appraisal process and the valuations.

The power also changed when Jean talked about Robby. She became very powerful in Mark's eyes because she had been the primary parent and it seemed to him as though he really didn't count at this point. Jean was afraid that Mark wouldn't care about Robby as much as he did in the past and that she had to protect Robby from the pain of losing his father.

The second session also went smoothly. The appraisals were in, and the business was more valuable than the house. They agreed that Jean would have the house and Mark would have his business. They each would have a car, and the other assets and liabilities were discussed and distributed on paper to consider. The miscellaneous furnishings and personal effects were discussed and tentatively divided. They then worked on their budgets, leading to the discussion of income and support issues. They found, as most couples do, that the present income was not sufficient to pay for all of the needs of two households. The next point of the discussion turned to Jean and her ability to earn income. Jean was very upset about this and asked that we defer discussion until the next session.

The power again moved from person to person, back and forth with the changing subjects and issues of discussion. Mark felt especially vulnerable when the business was valued at more than he expected, and still his earnings were not enough for the divorced family to live on. Jean was devastated at the suggestion of her earning an income. She had no idea where to begin and suggested that she could become a bag lady. This was not an unusual response of a frightened woman in mediation who has never worked outside of the home.

The third session began with a feeling of great tension in the room. The opening question, "Is there anything either of you wishes to say before we begin?" was met with a firm but soft "Yes" by Jean. When asked what she wanted to say, she said she wanted to ask Mark about "this" and pulled a Sucrets box out of her bag. Mark looked at it and sank in his chair, his face having fallen and his forehead buried in his hands. I had never before witnessed such power as that of the Sucrets box in a mediation session! When I asked her what this meant, she replied, "He knows," in a very firm, strong voice. Mark shook his head, looked up and with tears streaming down his face he said to her, "I'm sorry, I thought I was going to lose everything, and I just wanted something to start my business up again after the divorce."

I was still dumbfounded—after all, what did a Sucrets box have to do with his business? I asked Jean to explain all of this to me. She said she was going through the file drawer where he kept all of the family and business records to find a record of her car insurance. She insisted that she was not snooping, but that this was one of her homework assignments for the budget process. She said she found this Sucrets box and when she opened it she found $5,000.00 in it.

I asked Mark if that was correct. He nodded that it was, and apologized profusely, saying that it was stupid but he was so scared because he had already lost his home and his son and would probably lose his business; he thought if he just had something to start over again, he might make it. I asked Jean if she believed him and she did. I then asked him if he had any other money hidden and he said no.

We concluded the session, and they decided to wait a few weeks before the next session. About two weeks later Jean called and said that they had returned to their marriage therapist to try to put the marriage back together. If it did not work they would return to mediation to finish the divorce. They never called back.

CONCLUSION

Power moved between Jean and Mark, as it did with the others. They each perceived it differently than the reality, because they often saw themselves as vulnerable and the other as powerful. Power in the negotiation and mediation of a divorce is not as great a force as perceived, and it seldom has the influence that attorneys and others attribute to it. For mediators, it needs to be identified and managed within the context of mediation. The need for power is grounded in insecurity, and it is often used out of desperate necessity. Perhaps the most helpful thing that can be said about power is that it exists most significantly in the eyes of the beholder.

8

Strategies to
Avoid Impasse

The course of bargaining and negotiations is never the same for any couple. Some couples may be able to reach cooperative agreements quite easily, while other couples constantly appear on the brink of disaster or impasse when in mediation. The following "impasse strategies" show that the skills employed by an experienced divorce mediator follow a logical pattern and are consistent with the conceptual framework discussed in Chapter One.

Impasse strategies represent identifiable intervention techniques that are used to increase the chances of settlement. The techniques are not simply used randomly, but as a general rule are employed more toward the latter stages of the process than in the beginning. Most divorce mediation cases average eight to 10 hours of in-session mediation time and the majority of these intervention strategies would be used during the last half of the process time.

As with any technique used by a mediator, it is not so much a question of whether it works, but rather what is learned by trying the technique. That is, cases often settle more easily when everyone in the room clearly knows what is causing the disagreement and in some instances the impasse strategy is used as a method of determining which roadblock is truly preventing a settlement. In other instances, the impasse strategy can create an important turning point in the discussions, allowing a couple to see more clearly the nature of their dispute and what must be done to achieve settlement.

Unfortunately, it is not possible to read the box score at the end of mediation and determine how the negotiations were played and what contributed most to cooperative resolution of the conflict. The parties themselves are often unable to point to any single factor that helped them reach agreement, and the success of the divorce mediation process is more tied to the impact of all the steps and strategies. However, just as any skilled trial attorney wants to be overprepared, a good family mediator should have an overabundance of skills to employ, even if it is difficult to determine which are most appropriate to a particular case or situation.

The list on the next page is a summary of the various strategies to be discussed in detail.

1. Start Over Again
2. Delay Discussion of the Disputed Issue and Work on Other Matters
3. Use an Expert
4. Caucus Separately
5. Approach Problem from Radically Different Perspective (Shake up the Gameboard)
6. Ask Them to Experiment with Several Options Before Reaching Agreement
7. Refer to a Therapist for Joint Counseling Around Emotions of Divorce
8. Discuss Fairness
9. Suggest That Some Issues Can Never Be Rationally Decided, They Must Simply Be Decided
10. Request That the Children Attend a Mediation Session
11. Request a Second Opinion from Another Attorney
12. Conduct a Five-Party Meeting with Both Attorneys Present
13. Comment on the Give-and-Take Score
14. Discuss the Sanity Factor
15. Focus on the Future Rather Than on the Past

1. START OVER AGAIN

Often the first impasse intervention to use when all the usual procedural steps have been followed is to repeat the steps in an abbreviated fashion. Although the mediator certainly will know more about the couple's conflict at this point, this intervention technique is most useful when the mediator cannot determine exactly what is causing the impasse or slow progress. The technique is analogous to what a pilot does when the airplane won't start—go back to the beginning and start the preflight checklist again. Similarly, a skilled mediator employing a process theory of mediation goes back to square one and runs through a checklist of steps with the couple because it is always the process (and not the mediator) that works to solve the conflict. When repeating the steps in a more abbreviated fashion, the mediator and the couple can often locate and resolve the problem that is causing impasse.

Agreement to Begin Mediation

The purpose of this step is a reexamination of the initial commitment made by the couple to begin mediation. The goal is to strengthen cooperative attitudes or uncover negative attitudes such as suspicion or mistrust that may still exist and contribute to impasse. As pointed out in Chapter One, perhaps the most crucial indicators of success in any cooperative conflict resolution process are the attitudes held by the parties in the negotiations. During the latter stages of mediation discussions, a review of the commitment both initially made upon entering mediation can hopefully strengthen that cooperative commitment.

Most family mediators use a signed Agreement to Mediate form containing language stating that each agrees to be fair and equitable throughout the mediation process. The couple might be asked if they feel the other has been fair and equitable. Do they feel the mediator has been fair? These questions help determine whether one party might feel the other is using mediation for an improper purpose.

Obtaining Necessary Facts

Early in any mediation process, the parties will collect and exchange factual information. If impasse occurs during later negotiations, a question the mediator asks is whether or not more facts are needed. Since agreements and decisions are based upon factual information, the importance of this aspect of the process should not be overlooked. Frequently, parties in conflict disagree about some factual aspect of the case, but such disagreement is not apparent to either the parties or the mediator. Rechecking facts gives the mediator an opportunity to obtain clues about why they may be having settlement difficulties. In the case example of Dan and Linda (Chapter Three), a missing fact that became very important to the settlement was the need to obtain information about the tax effect of various levels of spousal support. When this important information was obtained, it became easier for the husband to agree to the amount of support the wife requested.

Defining Issues

If a review check assures that more facts will not be useful, the next step in the process is to determine whether or not the issues have been correctly defined. Since the way issues are defined may determine a cooperative outcome, unresolved issues should be scrutinized to see if a different definition of the issue will unlock the impasse. A good technique is to ask each to state what is the single most important issue or problem standing in the way of settlement, and if that issue or problem could be solved, would the case move towards agreement. Compare whether the issues stated at this point are the same as when the step was completed the first time early on in the mediation process.

Additionally, if the couple still defines issues in win-lose statements such as who will have the children, try to convince them that the issue is not who will own the children, but when each parent will have them. Attempting to state an issue in a way that permits a mutual solution rather than a win-lose solution will often help couples move off impasse.

Addressing Needs and Wants

Frequently, couples will be afraid or unable to state clearly what they need or want. They may state their needs in a way that deprives the other spouse of meeting his or her needs. A useful impasse strategy is to ask each spouse to very clearly state what is needed today to help settle the case. By listening to the answer, a mediator will obtain a clearer idea of the roadblocks to settlement. There are universal needs basic to all divorcing couples that, when met, seem to make the case less likely to reach impasse. These needs can be summarized as:

a. The need to continue to be good loving parents to the children in the future.
b. The need to have some measure of financial security, even though the process of terminating the marital partnership usually leaves one spouse in a better financial position.
c. The need to feel that the accumulated assets of the marriage have been divided in a fair manner consistent with principles of fairness that each agree to.

Refocusing on needs of the parties has the effect of encouraging couples to state clearly what will settle the case. By determining whether a basic need is not being met, the mediator will certainly learn more about whether the need is reasonable and whether it can be satisfied.

Brainstorm Again About Options

This step can often be the most useful step in the process of settlement negotiations. It involves not only generating new options, but also reviewing how previously proposed options will work. Frequently, an option presented by one side may be rejected even before the presenter has completed the description of the option. A technique used to prevent the premature dismissal of a useful option is to ask the parties to examine in detail how the option will work. For example, the couple may be asked not to reject any settlement option until all settlement options have been discussed. This phase of the review process will be expanded later in the discussion of specific impasse strategies designed to encourage the generation of new options.

2. DELAY DISCUSSION OF THE DISPUTED ISSUE AND WORK ON OTHER MATTERS

Experienced mediators know that sometimes an issue will not settle because the time is not right for it to settle. This impasse strategy relates to the role of the mediator as controller and manager of the process. As controller of the sequence of when issues are discussed, it is wise to refrain from forcing a settlement upon the couple. If some issue cannot be resolved when it is being discussed for the first time, it doesn't mean it will not settle; it usually means that it will have to be settled later. Timing is more important to the negotiation process than most people realize.

3. USE AN EXPERT

This impasse strategy attempts to ensure that decisions are based upon the best possible facts. Experts are used throughout the divorce process: to appraise property, to determine tax consequences, etc. Skilled mediators also make use of experts to assist in impasse situations such as custody and parenting. The use of a child psychiatrist or skilled family therapist can be just the device that is necessary to help the couple reach agreement on parenting. An example of this use is found in Chapter Three concerning the case of the husband whose wife refused to allow him to see the children in the presence of his girlfriend.

4. CAUCUS SEPARATELY

Meeting separately with each can be one method of finding out what is causing impasse. However, caucusing as a routine technique has its disadvantages because it causes mistrust and concern about what is being discussed separately. It can be effective after the mediator has gained the trust of the parties. Used sparingly, it is a technique for reducing the tensions in the room as well as learning from each of the parties some information that they may not wish to share in the presence of the other.

Within the profession of family mediation, there is disagreement about the propriety of using this technique since divorce is quite different from a labor-management mediation where caucusing is frequently employed. If it appears that the discussions are at a stalemate and caucusing is contemplated, first seek the permission of the parties to meet separately and establish whether or not the information given to the mediator must be shared with each or whether the information will be kept confidential by the mediator.

5. SHAKE UP THE GAMEBOARD

This impasse strategy is best described as throwing the Monopoly pieces in the air and starting over again. Sometimes it is necessary to ask the parties if it is possible to attack the problem from a completely different perspective. It requires the mediator to keep track of the avenues the couple has been traveling in their attempt to settle the case and to suggest that another route might provide settlement. Essentially, this strategy tries to get the couple to look at a completely different approach to solving the problem. It might entail the mediator asking the question of whether they have considered doing something that has not yet been discussed, such as selling the home, or experimenting with a different parenting exchange schedule.

One recent case where this technique worked to prevent impasse involved a couple who could not agree on who would move out of the house in order to accomplish a physical separation. After listening to them argue for over an hour about all the reasons each had for staying in the house, I said, "Why don't both of you move out?"

I proceeded to explain the concept of birdnesting which has the children stay in the house and Mom and Dad move in and out of the house, usually a week at a time. Many couples will rent a small efficiency apartment nearby and use it as the place where they each live when not at the house with the children. Both liked the idea because neither was given an advantage and it allowed both to experience what it was like living somewhere other than the family home.

6. ASK THEM TO EXPERIMENT WITH SEVERAL OPTIONS BEFORE REACHING AGREEMENT

This strategy is based upon the concept that settlement will occur more easily if there is permission to change the decision should one of the parties not be satisfied with the choice made. This impasse strategy is used more in the early stages of the mediation process and it asks simply that couples not put pressure on themselves to make permanent agreements, but rather learn to practice at their arrangements before the agreements are made final and binding. This strategy works best in the area of parenting schedules and allows the couple to reach temporary agreements that can later be changed.

An example is the couple at impasse over the question of whether the children should live primarily in one home or whether there should be approximately equal time-sharing in both homes. The mediator suggests that they try each of their proposed arrangements for one month and return to mediation in two months after experimenting with both proposals. The children's reaction to both schedules can also be appraised.

7. REFER TO A THERAPIST FOR JOINT COUNSELING
AROUND EMOTIONS OF DIVORCE

The process of divorce occurs on two levels. It occurs on a level of the things of the marriage and on an emotional level. The mediator helps the couple negotiate about the things of the marriage (children, money, property) and, usually, these negotiations can be therapeutic in the emotional area. However, an occasional couple will have great difficulty in mediation because they have not resolved the emotional aspects of the separation.

The most common example of this is when one spouse refuses to accept the separation or divorce. A skilled family therapist can take the couple through a process of marriage termination therapy which helps reduce the prospect of impasse. (It must be remembered that when a couple engages in mediation, one way for the less accepting spouse to resist divorce is to sabotage the mediation process by making outrageous demands or engage in blaming and fault-finding negotiating strategies.)

8. DISCUSS FAIRNESS

This strategy for avoiding impasse attempts to determine whether the couple is using the same definition of fairness. If they are not in agreement on a common definition of fairness, they will have difficulty reaching agreement on the particular issue in question. An example of this situation is the wife whose principle of fairness requires the husband to pay spousal support forever because she was faithful to the marital contract and he was not. If the husband employs a concept of fairness that says he should pay rehabilitative spousal support only until his wife completes retraining, they will tend to remain at impasse on the issue of length of spousal support.

A strategy to deal with differences in concepts of fairness is to first help them determine a mutual concept of fairness. The example above might appear to be difficult to mediate, but there are other principles of fairness that both might be willing to adopt. By accepting the fact that they may each continue to hold their beliefs, the mediator can assist them in moving to agreement about fairness by urging the wife to let go of blaming and fault-finding while at the same time helping the husband understand that women tend to earn much less than men and he may need to share his income for a longer period that he wants in order for her to become independent. Impasse may be avoided if they both agree to a new concept of fairness that says that each has the right to basic economic security after the divorce.

Although the discussions may consume time and energy around defining what is meant by basic economic security, at least the wife is no longer blaming the husband for violating his marriage vows and the husband is not trying to get her working immediately. A plan can be drawn to eventually allow her to become financially independent, but the mediator cannot possibly help decide the settlement implications of one spouse's infidelity.

9. SUGGEST THAT SOME ISSUES CAN NEVER BE RATIONALLY DECIDED, THEY MUST SIMPLY BE DECIDED

This technique allows the mediator to help a couple realize it is not necessary to agree on everything. For example, if the husband is Catholic and the wife Methodist, they will still need to decide how the children will be given religious instruction, even though they can't decide on which faith. This is the type of issue that can cause people a great deal of trouble unless they realize this problem would have surfaced even had they stayed married and, therefore, for the sake of the children, what is most needed is an answer. Either choice is not the wrong choice. The only wrong choice is continued conflict and inability to make the decision.

10. REQUEST THAT THE CHILDREN ATTEND A MEDIATION SESSION

In severe custody disputes, this can be a very useful technique to prevent impasse. While it is never desirable to permit the children to decide whom they will live with, bringing the children in at a working session can serve a useful purpose and can prevent the case from reaching impasse. The result of such a session is usually to show that the children do, in fact, care deeply about both parents. By giving them an opportunity for input, the children are able to talk privately with the mediator about their concerns (see Erickson & McKnight Erickson, 1986).

11. REQUEST A SECOND OPINION FROM ANOTHER ATTORNEY

Frequently, a cause of impasse is the advice given to one of the spouses by his or her attorney. Should one party's attorney make unrealistic predictions about the potential outcome of litigation, this will cause that spouse to make unreasonable demands in the mediation room. The mediator can ask that spouse first to obtain a written guarantee that the outcome in court will be as predicted. Since such a guarantee will not be obtained, the request serves as an opportunity to suggest that a second opinion be obtained from another attorney concerning the likelihood of such an outcome. Concurrent with this, the mediator must also focus on the needs of the unrealistic spouse in order to help the person decide whether or not the advice of the attorney is sound advice. In some cases, the client may need to sort out the conflicting recommendations of two attorneys and, ultimately, the client must decide whether or not the settlement is fair and meets basic needs.

12. CONDUCT A FIVE-PARTY MEETING WITH BOTH ATTORNEYS PRESENT

Contrary to popular belief, the presence of the spouses' attorneys in the room can actually help facilitate a settlement, even if one or both of the attorneys are zealous litigators. The mediator uses the attorneys' presence to show the absurdity of the litigation process. Since neither attorney can predict with certainty what the outcome in court will be, the parties have an opportunity to assess each attorney's competence, as well as to hear the answer to the one prediction that can be answered with certainty—the cost of a trial litigated on all of the issues. Upon hearing the answer to this question, couples will usually ask their attorneys to assist them in settling the case.

Where both attorneys are supportive of the mediation process, the sessions can actually save time in the final processing of the case. Additionally, it is much easier for the mediator to impose reality when an attorney leans over to one of the spouses and says, "I think you have a great deal of exposure on this issue and perhaps the settlement should be seriously considered." The mediator may wish to say something like that, but it is much more effective when an attorney does so.

13. COMMENT ON THE GIVE-AND-TAKE SCORE

This is a form of intervention that prevents impasse by reminding the couple that they have made considerable progress. Parties in difficult negotiations will often be so consumed by their own efforts that they forget to observe the concessions made by the other side. The mediator keeps track of progress and can point out to the spouses that they have both made a great deal of progress towards settlement. This strategy can also be effective in getting the more rigid spouse to move away from a strongly held position.

14. DISCUSS THE SANITY FACTOR

In most complicated negotiations, but particularly around divorce, it is not possible to achieve perfection. If the couple's marital estate exceeds $400,000.00 and each will receive approximately $200,000.00 of property, it makes little sense to fight over a $250.00 stained glass window. This intervention can also be used in the case of impasse over length and amount of spousal support. Suppose the husband will agree to pay spousal support of $1,500.00 a month for four years and the wife wants $1,500.00 per month for seven years. They really are not far apart if this couple also has a $400,000.00 net worth, because $36,000.00 more of alimony needs to be discounted to a present value to account for its lessened value due to the taxes owed and it not being received until six or seven years later.

Therefore, suppose an accountant tells them that the present value of the right to receive $18,000.00 per year six years from now is really worth $14,000.00 today. (That is, $14,000.00 deposited today at average interest rates would earn enough to fund the monthly payments in years six and seven.) The $14,000.00 impasse represents less than 4% of the entire marital estate to be divided, and it would be insane to have this as an impasse when they are so close to settling the case. With the mediator's intervention in pointing out the sanity factor, this couple might decide to have a slightly unequal division of property allowing for the wife to receive 54% of the $400,000.00 and the husband to receive 46%.

15. FOCUS ON THE FUTURE RATHER THAN ON THE PAST

In some cases, the past can become so tangled that although significant time in the mediation sessions is allowed for unsorting the past, it becomes impossible to ever obtain agreement on what happened. An example of this surfaced recently in a case involving a couple who had been separated for three years and actively involved in litigation for over two years. During the time the case was slowly working its way through the court system, the husband was given permission to sell several marital assets. He also tried to sell out of a marginally successful real estate partnership, but could not and eventually ended up dumping more money into this venture. Trying to trace the tangled web of transactions proved very difficult. In the end, approximately $10,000.00 could not be properly accounted for. Both agreed that most of the missing money ended up in the real estate partnership.

As they continued to angrily fight about whose idea it was to invest in the real estate venture, I interrupted them, saying, "We'll never be able to completely unscramble the past and you only have so much money left to divide. What do you each need to get a proper start for the future?" This intervention focused them back on the task of unhooking what now existed and the case was settled during the remainder of the session.

CONCLUSION

This listing of impasse strategies is by no means exhaustive. However, each intervention has successfully led to changing the course of the negotiations in many cases. Likewise, each strategy has occasionally resulted in absolutely no movement toward settlement. Such techniques do not guarantee success, but they do increase the chances for moving the couple toward a cooperative settlement, and they pose no negative risk to the process.

Appendix A

Rules and Guidelines of Family Mediation Services

Effect of Rules and Guidelines

The purpose of these rules is to assist you in reaching a settlement of the issues submitted for mediation. The rules and guidelines are necessary to protect the integrity and confidentiality of the mediation process. The guidelines will assist you in examining relevant factors necessary for a full discussion of the issues. You will determine a resolution of your conflict, and these rules will not be used other than to protect the integrity of the process and to ensure full discussion and analysis of relevant issues.

Agreement to Mediate

These rules will be a part of the mediation agreement whenever the agreement provides or whenever you have agreed in writing that mediation shall be conducted by Family Mediation Services, Inc. These rules and any amendments shall apply in this form at the time the mediation is initiated.

Conduct of Mediation

The mediation process may be conducted by the mediator(s) in whatever manner will most expeditiously permit full discussion and resolution of the issues. The mediator(s) is authorized to negotiate between you and to encourage you to settle each issue.

Concurrence of Mediator(s)

The mediator(s) may indicate to you his/her concurrence or nonconcurrence with the settlement decisions you have made. Only in those cases where the mediator does not concur with your intended settlement decisions will there be a statement of nonconcurrence. The comments of the mediator will be contained in the Memorandum of Agreement and only in those cases where the mediator feels the couple has been unfair to each other will a comment be made about the nature of the mediator's concern and the reasons for such nonconcurrence.

Although legislation is pending in the state of Minnesota that would make mediation protected by the confidentiality statutes, at present it is not in effect. Therefore, we ask that each couple contract with each other and with Family Mediation Services to keep the mediation discussions confidential. By signing the Agreement to Mediate which incorporates these rules and guidelines, we are asking you to agree as follows:

(a) Mediation is a procedure for reaching settlement of a dispute either in litigation or likely to be in litigation between you.

(b) Through the adoption of these rules, you agree that neither of you may call either the mediator(s) or any officer or agent of the Family Mediation Services as a witness in any litigation of any description in which they are called upon to testify as to any matter regarding the mediation proceeding; and, in like manner, both of you shall be stopped from requiring the production in such a litigation of any records or documents or any other notes or papers made by the mediator(s) of Family Mediation Services.

(c) The foregoing exclusions from evidence and exemptions of the mediator(s) and parties from giving testimony or being called upon to produce documents shall apply also to the use of neutral experts and other professionals called upon by you in mediation.

(d) Mediations conducted by a professional mediator shall come within the purview of his/her professional privilege as established by the Academy of Family Mediators and any other statutory protection enacted after the date of these rules.

Full Disclosure

Each person shall fully disclose in the presence of the other all information and writings, such as financial statements, income tax returns, etc., as requested by the mediators(s) and all information requested by the opposite party if the mediator(s) find such other disclosure is appropriate to the mediation process and may aid you in reaching a settlement. At the conclusion of the mediation process, you may find that the attorneys will request further verification and disclosure in order to aid their review and implementation of your decisions in mediation.

Preparation of Budgets

The preparation of budgets by each of you is an essential part of the mediation process. If either of you fails or refuses to prepare a budget adequately reflecting his/her needs, the mediator(s) shall have the duty to suspend mediation of these issues, or, at their discretion, declare an impasse.

Participation of Children and Others

Children or other persons having a direct interest in the mediation may participate in mediation sessions related to their interest with consent of the parties and the mediator(s).

Transfers of Property

During the mediation process, neither of you will transfer, encumber, conceal, or in any other way dispose of marital assets except in the usual course of business or for the necessities of life. Transactions by either party in the regular course of business and for any other purpose affecting 10% or more of the total assets will require prior mutual agreement and the agreement of your attorneys if you are represented at the time of entering mediation.

Drafting of Memorandum of Agreement

The mediator, at the conclusion of the mediation sessions, shall draft a detailed memorandum setting forth the decisions agreed upon by you in mediation. The Memorandum of Agreement shall contain background information about the parties and shall set forth the factual information relied upon by the parties in reaching settlement. The Memorandum of Agreement will be submitted by each of you to your attorneys who will review and implement your decisions as reflected in the Memorandum. Any new or omitted issues raised by your attorneys shall be returned to mediation should they be unable to efficiently and cooperatively resolve such new or omitted issues.

Legal Representation

You understand that the mediator(s) does not represent either or both of you. Effective legal representation is required, and you each agree to retain counsel of your own choice to represent you no later than at the conclusion of the mediation process. Family Mediation Services recommends that you retain legal representation at the time you commence the mediation process. This recommendation is based upon the fact that the role of the attorneys in reviewing and implementing your decisions is an important role that can allow for an expedited completion of the divorce process if you have selected your attorneys during the mediation process. This also eliminates confusion about your legal rights as the mediator(s) does not discuss legal issues nor your legal rights in mediation.

You will rather be expected to discuss and negotiate a settlement based upon your own standards of fairness and your own decisions about what is best for yourself and your family.

Family Mediation Services maintains a panel of attorneys who are familiar with the divorce process and, if you wish, the list is available. You are still required to interview and choose your own attorney who will respect the work you have completed in mediation and who will provide you with an independent judgment of your decisions.

The amendment of the rules will be at such time as to not interfere with the mediation process. Family Mediation Services reserves the right to amend these rules at any time, provided, however, such amendment shall not apply to existing controversies which are in mediation on the date of such amendments.

Appendix B

Agreement to Begin Mediation

This AGREEMENT TO BEGIN MEDIATION is signed by the parties and Family Mediation Services, Inc., to create and clarify the mediation relationship.

The parties desire to mediate all issues which might be involved in contested litigation. The parties agree to abide by the Rules and Guidelines of Family Mediation Services, Inc. This agreement reflects each party's sincere intention to be fair and equitable during mediation.

IN CONSIDERATION OF THE ABOVE:

1. Family Mediation Services, Inc., will conduct the mediation and will be compensated at the rate of $__ per hour for actual mediation sessions. Payment for mediation sessions will be made at the conclusion of each mediation session.
2. In addition to compensation for mediation sessions,

Family Mediation Services, Inc., will bill up to three hours ($___) for time spent by the mediator outside of the actual sessions.

All parties agree that legal advice and legal representation is not part of mediation and will not be provided by Family Mediation Services, Inc. Legal advice is not given in mediation sessions and the parties agree that legal issues created by their decisions reached in mediation will be referred to their attorneys. Each party agrees to retain legal counsel prior to implementing the decisions reached in mediation.

By signing this agreement each party acknowledges receipt of a copy of the Rules and Guidelines of Family Mediation Services, Inc., which are incorporated as a part of this Agreement to Begin Mediation.

This AGREEMENT TO BEGIN MEDIATION is signed by the parties and by Family Mediation Services, Inc., this _____ day of _____, 19___.

FAMILY MEDIATION SERVICES, INC.

By_____   _____

_____   _____

Appendix C

Family Mediation Services Questionnaire

INSTRUCTIONS: Please provide all of the following information to the best of your ability, even though it may duplicate what other party may provide.

1. Full name _____ Birthdate _____
   Street Address _____ Home Phone _____
   City _____ State _____ County _____ Zip _____
   Workplace _____ Work Address _____
   City _____ State _____ Zip ____ Work Phone _____ Ext. __
   Continuous residence in Minnesota since _____
2. Other Party's name _____ Birthdate _____
   Street Address _____ Home Phone _____
   City _____ State _____ County _____ Zip _____
   Workplace _____ Work Address _____
   City _____ State _____ Zip ____ Work Phone _____ Ext. __
3. Marriage Date _____ Place _____
4. CHILDREN:

Full Name:	Birthdate:	Age:	Living with:
_____	_____	_____	_____
_____	_____	_____	_____
_____	_____	_____	_____
_____	_____	_____	_____
_____	_____	_____	_____

5. Are you and the other party living together? ___no ___yes If not, please give the date of separation: _____
6. Are you employed? _____ Employer _____ Since _____ Position _____ Employed since _____ Salary _____ H.S. Diploma _____ Degree/Certificates _____ Major/Year _____ Continuous employment since _____
7. Is your spouse employed? ____ Employer _____ Since ____ Position _____ Employed since _____ Salary _____ Educational status _____ Continuous employment since _____
8. List all prior marriages. (Include name of prior spouse, and how, when and where prior marriages were terminated.) _____
9. List names and ages of any children of any prior marriage and state with whom such children live. _____
10. Do you have an interest in reconciliation? _____
11. Is there a dispute about the custody of the children? _____
12. Attorney's name _____ Phone _____ Address _____
13. Should creditors be notified? _____
14. Do you have a will? _____ Should it be reviewed? _____
15. Are there joint bank acounts to which your spouse has access? ____
16. Does your spouse have credit cards for which you are responsible? _____ If yes, specify _____
17. Who referred you to Family Mediation Services? _____
18. Have you had marriage or family counseling? _____ If yes, with whom? _____
19. Are you presently in therapy or counseling? _____ If yes, with whom? _____
20. Date you filled out this form: _____

ASSETS AND LIABILITIES

Please list the value of each of the following items of property. If you are unable to obtain the exact present value, estimate what you think the value may be. If any item is located in a state other than that in which you live, indicate where such item is located, and if necessary, give details on a separate sheet. Please indicate items acquired by gift, inheritance, or prior to marriage by marking with a star(*).

Be sure to list the names and account numbers of all of the items, and the legal descriptions of real estate. This information is important in identifying the items, and is necessary for inclusion in your legal papers.

LIST THE ESTIMATED VALUE IN THE COLUMN IN WHOSE NAME THE ITEM IS HELD

Assets:

	Husband	*Wife*	*Joint*

A. Bank names and account numbers:

B. Accounts receivable, notes:

C. Stocks and bonds:

D. Real estate: Legal description

E. Life insurance: Please list name of company, policy number, face value and cash value—use a separate sheet, if necessary.

_____   _____ _____ _____
_____   _____ _____ _____

Where are the policies located? _____

F. Business interests: Please furnish last balance sheet and P & L statement, tax return, buy-sell agreements, etc.

_____   _____ _____ _____
_____   _____ _____ _____
_____   _____ _____ _____

G. Miscellaneous property (patents, trademarks, copyrights, royalties—please furnish last statement and descriptive booklet—stock options, etc.):

_____   _____ _____ _____
_____   _____ _____ _____
_____   _____ _____ _____

H. Automobiles, special personal property:

_____   _____ _____ _____
_____   _____ _____ _____
_____   _____ _____ _____
_____   _____ _____ _____

I. Pension and profit-sharing plans (please furnish last statement and descriptive booklet). [IRAs, KEOGH, and other retirement plans]

_____   _____ _____ _____
_____   _____ _____ _____
_____   _____ _____ _____

J. Personal property, furnishings, etc.

_____   _____ _____ _____
_____   _____ _____ _____
_____   _____ _____ _____
_____   _____ _____ _____

K. Income tax refunds—Amount due:
   State _____   _____ _____ _____
   IRS _____   _____ _____ _____

Liabilities:
A. Mortages on real estate: *Husband*   *Wife*   *Joint*

_____   _____ _____ _____
_____   _____ _____ _____
_____   _____ _____ _____

B. Notes to banks and others:

_____ _____ _____ _____
_____ _____ _____ _____
_____ _____ _____ _____
_____ _____ _____ _____

C. Other debts (medical, dental, charge accounts, etc.):

_____ _____ _____ _____
_____ _____ _____ _____
_____ _____ _____ _____
_____ _____ _____ _____

D. Taxes due:

_____ _____ _____ _____
_____ _____ _____ _____
_____ _____ _____ _____

BUDGETS

Income:	*Husband*	*Wife*
Gross salary	_____	_____
Dividend income	_____	_____
Interest income	_____	_____
Income from trusts	_____	_____
Rental income	_____	_____
Pension	_____	_____
Social security	_____	_____
Other income (describe):	_____	_____
_____	_____	_____
_____	_____	_____
_____	_____	_____
TOTAL GROSS ANNUAL INCOME	_____	_____
ANNUAL TAXES	_____	_____
NET ANNUAL INCOME	_____	_____
NET AVERAGE MONTHLY INCOME	_____	_____

Monthly Expenses:		
ITEM	*SELF*	*CHILDREN*
Housing (Rent, PITI)	_____	_____
Household insurance	_____	_____
Maintenance	_____	_____
Replacement of household items	_____	_____

Other (specify) _____   _____   _____
Food, household supplies and lunches
  at work   _____   _____
Clothing   _____   _____
Medical and dental:
  Medical insurance   _____   _____
  Medical bills not covered by insur-
    ance   _____   _____
  Dental insurance   _____   _____
  Dental bills not covered by insur-
    ance   _____   _____
  Medicines and drugs   _____   _____
Transportation:
  Auto payments   _____   _____
  Auto gas and oil   _____   _____
  Auto maintenance/repairs   _____   _____
  Auto insurance   _____   _____
  Auto license   _____   _____
Parking   _____   _____
Other (bus fare, taxis, etc.)   _____   _____
Other motorized vehicles (boat, plane, cycle, snowmobile, truck, etc.):
  Payments   _____   _____
  Fuel   _____   _____
  Maintenance/repairs   _____   _____
  Insurance   _____   _____
  License   _____   _____
  Other   _____   _____
Recreation   _____   _____
Insurance: _____   _____
  Life insurance   _____   _____
  Disability insurance   _____   _____
  Other (specify) _____   _____   _____
Utilities:
  Electricity   _____   _____
  Gas/heating oil   _____   _____
  Telephone   _____   _____
  Water   _____   _____
  Domestic services   _____   _____
  Garbage/trash   _____   _____
  Yard maintenance/snow removal   _____   _____
Incidentals:
  Drugstore items   _____   _____

Books, magazines, newspapers	_____	_____
Haircuts	_____	_____
Gifts	_____	_____
Other (specify) _____		
_____	_____	_____
Dry cleaning/laundromat	_____	_____
Dues (professional, union)	_____	_____
Private school tuition (children)	_____	_____
College tuition (spouse)	_____	_____
Transportation (re: school)	_____	_____
Books	_____	_____
Other	_____	_____
Allowances—children	_____	_____
Nursery school	_____	_____
Day care	_____	_____
Vacations	_____	_____
Charities and church	_____	_____
Pet expenses	_____	_____
Other (specify) _____	_____	_____
_____		
Income taxes	_____	_____
TOTAL MONTHLY NEED	_____	_____
TOTAL MONTHLY NET INCOME	_____	_____
OVERAGE/SHORTFALL	_____	_____

References

Barker, R. L. *Treating Couples in Crisis*. New York: The Free Press, 1984.

Bercovitch, J. *Social Conflicts and Third Parties: Strategies of Conflict Resolution*. Boulder, CO: Westview Press, 1984.

Bolton, R. *People Skills*. Englewood Cliffs, NJ: Prentice-Hall, 1979.

Deschner, J. P. *The Hitting Habit*. New York: The Guilford Press, 1983.

Deutsch, M. *The Resolution of Conflict: Constructive and Destructive Processes*. New Haven, CT: Yale University Press, 1973.

Erickson, S., & McKnight Erickson, M. *Child Custody Mediation Manual*. Minneapolis: Erickson Mediation Institute, 1986.

Fisher, R., & Ury, W. *Getting to Yes: Negotiating Agreement Without Giving In*. New York: Houghton Mifflin, 1981.

Folberg, J., & Taylor, A. *Mediation: A Comprehensive Guide to Resolving Conflicts Without Litigation*. San Francisco, CA: Jossey-Bass, 1984.

Gelles, R. J. *The Violent Home: A Study of Physical Aggression Between Husbands and Wives*. London: Sage Publications, 1972.

Giles-Sims, J. *Wife Battering*. New York: The Guilford Press, 1983.

Glasser, W. *Control Theory*. New York: Harper & Row, 1984.

Kaslow, F., & Schwartz, L. *The Dynamics of Divorce: A Life Cycle Perspective*. New York: Brunner/Mazel, 1987.

Kelly, J. Mediation and adversarial divorce: Initial findings from the divorce and mediation project. Unpublished paper, 1986.

Kressel, K. *The Process of Divorce*. New York: Basic Books, 1985.

Lefcourt, C. Women, mediation and family law. *Clearinghouse Review*, July, 1984.

Louisiana Civil Code, Article 160.

Minuchin, S. *Family Kaleidoscope*. Cambridge, MA: Harvard University Press, 1984.

Ricci, I. *Mom's House, Dad's House: Making Shared Custody Work*. New York: Macmillan, 1980.

Rogers, C. *Client-Centered Therapy*. Boston: Houghton Mifflin, 1951.

Roy, M. *Battered Women*. New York: Van Nostrand Reinhold, 1977.

Sander, F. Varieties of dispute processing. *Federal Rules Decisions*, Vol. 20, p. 122, 1976.

Wallerstein, J., Kelly, J. *Surviving the Breakup: How Children and Parents Cope with Divorce*. New York: Basic Books, 1980.

Watkins, C. *Victims, Aggressors and the Family Secret*. St. Paul, MN: Minnesota Department of Public Welfare, 1982.

Weitzman, L. *The Divorce Revolution*. New York: The Free Press, 1985.

Index